drive drunk, walk sober

ONE MAN'S STORY OF RECOVERY FROM THE GUILT
AND SHAME OF CAUSING A FATAL ACCIDENT
THROUGH DRUNK DRIVING.

By Sean Lynott

To Paul,

I am deeply sorry.

Your time stranded between day and night was brief.

May your short life further unfold in spirit.

To my Mother, Father, and aunt Agnes,

Thank you for the sheltered harbour where my shipwrecked soul could recuperate and set sail once more.

Copyright © 2017 by Sean Lynott.

All rights reserved. This book or any portion thereof may not be reproduced or used in any manner whatsoever without the express written permission of the publisher except for the use of brief quotations in a book review.

Publishing Services provided by Paper Raven Books

Printed in the United States of America

First Printing, 2017

Ebook ISBN 978-1-9998207-0-1
Paperback ISBN 978-1-9998207-1-8

This is a work of creative nonfiction. All names and identifying details have been changed to protect the privacy of the people involved. The events are portrayed to the best of the author's memory, which may indeed be flawed. If the author could not remember the exact words said by certain people or exact descriptions of certain things, he has retold them here in a way that evokes the feeling and meaning he experienced. This story is meant to portray the author's experience and no one else's experience.

This is my true story of alcoholism, causing the death of a young boy in a drunk driving accident, and the twenty years of recovery it would take to learn to live again.

My vision is to give you hope, that if you've been involved in a fatal accident due to alcoholism or any addiction, you can once again find a life worth living, a life worth loving.

I have created a community of people like us, who live with the memory of causing the death of someone yet live one day at a time. We believe that by being vulnerable and sharing what happened to us, we will touch the aching hearts of others and inspire them to come forward, get the help they need and deserve, love and forgive themselves, and start living life once more.

Whether the fatal accident was yesterday or a lifetime ago, we welcome you to join us, here:

www.seanlynott.com

In these pages are my story, and I'll look forward to hearing your story soon,

Sean Lynott

table of contents

Chapter 1
The Night That Would Haunt Me — 1

Chapter 2
Consequences — 25

Chapter 3
On the Run — 33

Chapter 4
The Serial Drunk Driver — 39

Chapter 5
The Seed Had Been Planted — 47

Chapter 6
The Accident — 55

Chapter 7
Turning Point — 59

Chapter 8
The Toxic Shame Game — 73

Chapter 9
A Message of Hope — 89

Finding the Help You Need — 93

chapter 1

The Night That Would Haunt Me

I awoke to an unfamiliar sound vibrating through my head. My stomach churned, and my body ached all over. This was my usual morning wake up call, except this time there was a new noise. I could hardly make out the squeaky, irritating sound at first. I soon realised it was a small transistor radio, belting out tunes that crackled with static, sounding alien to me at first.

My head was pounding, which was unusual; booze rarely gave me headaches. I raised my hand to my forehead, only to feel something like threads sticking out. So, I tugged at them and boy, did they hurt. That's when I realised they were stitches. I slowly touched my face and head feeling for more of these stitches, and found many others. They were over my right eye, my forehead, and in the back of my head. I could also feel something in my hair and picked out some of the sticky lumps, only to realise it was dried blood.

drive drunk, walk sober

The feeling of dread in my stomach was sickening, like a tight ball interwoven with strands of anxiety. I was trembling as I realised I was in a hospital bed. The distant noise was coming from a small radio. I tried to get up, but my body refused to obey. Usually, I would hop up from bed and look out of the window to see if my vehicle was there. This time, I just had an awful feeling in my gut that I had done some serious damage.

As I lay there in my hospital bed, I tried desperately to piece together what had happened the night before. Nothing would surface; typical of my blackout drinking. I would rarely ever remember what happened the night before, but this time I had a feeling something awful had happened. The news came on the radio, and the excited voice became very clear to me. There had been a fatal accident near Ballymire the night before with one boy killed, and his brother and the driver of the car seriously injured.

My heart started racing; pounding like jungle drums, and I thought it was going to beat its way out of my chest. I remember praying to God that I wasn't the one who had caused that accident. The nurse appeared in the ward and came over to me. I asked her if I was in that accident, and she confirmed that I was. *No, no, no!* I felt like jumping through the third story window. I was shocked. I couldn't believe it was me, yet I knew the truth. My body vibrating by that point, I started screaming and crying. There was so much noise running riot in my head. *Oh my God, oh my God!* I thought, as panic set in.

The little boy in me wanted his daddy to pick him up and hold him. I felt totally alone, frightened, and regretful. I think I was in a state of shock, because everything seemed to be in slow motion. Even though the nurse had confirmed my worst feelings, I tried to convince myself that it wasn't me. "Please,

God, please let it not be me," I cried. I just couldn't accept it. I thought of the families involved and couldn't imagine how they must have felt. And no words could accurately describe my emotional state that morning. Fear, guilt, remorse, sadness, bewilderment, frustration, despair, hopelessness, shame, self-pity, and anger ran wild like my brain was Grand Central Station. What would I do? How would I get through this? I couldn't stop trembling and crying, so the nurse gave me medication to calm me down. She pulled the curtain around the bed to leave me with my cocktail of misery and pain. As I laid back on the bed surrounded by the security of the cream coloured curtain, the voices in the ward became distant, my eyelids grew heavy, and I fell back to sleep.

Sometime later, I awoke to the sound of my mother's voice. "Sean, Sean wake up." At first, I thought she was calling me for school then suddenly remembered I was in the hospital and the nurse was telling me what happened, and my stomach felt sick with fear. I could hear her clearly but didn't want to open my eyes. I hoped it was just a bad dream; *please, God, tell me I'm dreaming and I just have to get up for school.* However, when I opened my eyes, it wasn't a dream, it was a nightmare. My heart sank, Yes, it was very real. I felt so ashamed of myself, like the greatest piece of shit to ever stand in two shoes, and as I looked at my father's face I felt a ball of fear, shame, and guilt in the pit of my stomach.

He looked sad and tired. I had let him down again, and this time it was dire. I said, "I'm so sorry, Dad, for all of this." He didn't know what to say. The guilt and shame I felt were almost overwhelming. Then, out of the blue he said, "I'm sure it wasn't your fault, Astór." He said he'd passed by the accident and that my van was on the proper side of the road. I think

drive drunk, walk sober

it was just his way of not accepting what had happened, or for taking my side as he sometimes did when I'd done wrong. For a moment, a feeling of relief and hope raced through my mind—maybe it wasn't my fault after all—only to fade away as quickly as it came.

I knew I was at fault, and I could no longer look either of my dear parents in the face. I just wanted to crawl under the bedclothes and die; to just disappear so I couldn't hurt them or anyone else ever again. I was well aware I'd caused a lot of hurt and pain for years, as a result of my alcoholism, but seemed powerless to get away from its clutches. Deep down, I was a good, caring, loving person. That was smothered by my alcoholism. My negative, all-consuming mind told me I was a scumbag and no good for anything. There was nothing left to say, but what could any of us say? There were no answers; just an awkward silence within the hospital bed curtain that day. It was so silent, it was screaming. I wanted to just disappear into thin air to escape. If I'd have had drink that moment, it would have gone down well.

Paul's funeral took place the following day, and I was still in the hospital. I couldn't bear to think of what I had done in a drunken blackout. I would not allow myself to think about it, as it was too awful to contemplate. I remember, I would try and replace the thought of that with thoughts of starting a new, sober life from then on. "I am never ever going to touch another drop of alcohol as long as I live." This hopeful plan would give me a few minutes' respite from my guilt and shame. Then, oh my God, I thought of that young boy being buried because of my drinking, and I would become overwhelmed.

How could his family, or myself, ever recover from this? A black cloud of depression began to descend upon me. I felt I was sinking deeper and deeper into an abyss. How could I ever accept this disaster, or even learn to live with it? How could Paul's family manage to go on after losing their young son? If only I could turn the clock back. If only I had never picked up alcohol. I wondered if there was there anything I could do for them to ease their pain. I thought the best thing I could do was to commit suicide or stay well away from them; to crawl into the nearest hole.

The day after Paul's funeral, I was told I could go home. I didn't want to go and face the reality of what had happened, but I had nowhere else to go. Here I was at twenty-four years of age, running back home yet again after one more disaster. This was a pattern of mine since I'd left school and started working. I would start a new job, get on well in the beginning, then get sacked for some alcohol related offence and have to return home to the safety and security of my parents. It was like I'd never been weaned off my parents' and never emotionally matured. I was like a twelve-year-old boy going on twenty-five. Every time I got a new job and rebooted my life, I resembled a small boy with a bundle of food tied upon the end of a stick, running away from home hoping to start a new life, but also being terrified at the thought of leaving the shelter of home. Looking back, I was immature. I'd stopped maturing at a young age and turned at first to cigarettes to cope with reality—and then to alcohol.

I didn't have any money saved up, as I drank every penny I earned, so there was nowhere to go except home to my parents' house.

drive drunk, walk sober

My father came to the hospital to take me home. It was a long, silent journey home. Nothing was said, and nothing could be said at that stage. It was just heart-breaking. I remember sitting next to him in the car, my heart pounding, emotions welling and wanting to express themselves. They were of shame, yet also love, of desperately wanting to tell him how much I loved him, wanting to throw my arms around him and say how so sorry I was for bringing all this hurt upon him and our family. But he was not a man for talking about emotions, and fear of rejection locked me down so the words just wouldn't come out. I desperately wanted to tell him of my struggle with alcohol but I knew he couldn't understand as he was a normal drinker. There was this invisible wedge between us. There was nothing I could say that would change anything, anyway. I didn't realise I was suffering from a fatal disease at that stage, so I just hammered myself with guilt and punishment.

Gone were the days when I couldn't wait to get out of school and run home to my father to help him on the farm. He taught me all about nature and animals, he was my hero and my best friend, and I loved him more than anything else in this world. Now, I felt I had hurt and disappointed him so bad. The little boy inside me couldn't even look at him, I felt so ashamed. I wished he would shout and scream at me or beat me, but no, there was nothing but an eerie silence between us. It was like we were a million miles apart now, and the wedge of alcoholism had driven us apart.

As we travelled along the little roads, hundreds of thoughts ran riot in my head.

Was it really my fault? Maybe Dad was right. No, no, you scumbag, you killed that boy and destroyed his family and really hurt Michael Walshe, the driver. What the fuck is wrong with you? Oh, my God! Why are you drinking? Don't you know it doesn't suit you? How many times have you to be told? Are you stupid or something when you continue to drink? Are you crazy? You're finished now, and you can never ever show your face around this area again. You better get out of this place. You don't deserve to be alive after what you've done. Why the hell didn't you die as well?

This voice was absolutely savage. If anyone else spoke to me like this voice, I would not tolerate it. This was to be my mantra for the next ten years. I used this as a stick to constantly beat myself. I was never going to forgive myself for this. It was just a constant horrible attack on myself. I just wanted to punish myself so severely as the drinking and now Paul's death clashed with every value I had within me since I was a child. This was ideal victim fodder for my self-pity, and then there were rare times when I would find a little compassion and say to myself, "*Sure this was an accident. When you left the pub that evening, you didn't intend to cause that crash. You are a good man; a kind, caring, and loving person.*" These were things I valued as a child. However, they melted away fast, like snow in springtime, and I would usually return to the default setting of beating myself to pieces, feeding the feeling of shame, gnawing self-pity, and guilt that was growing by the day.

We finally arrived home, and all my brothers and sisters were there. I came from a good, hard working, respectable family of four boys and four girls, from a small farming village in the west of Ireland. Everyone knew each other for miles around. I was the second born and also the black sheep. As I entered the house, I bowed my head down in shame. I could hardly look at my younger brothers and sisters. What could I do or say now? There was nothing but silence. I was guilty, so what could be said? I felt like a battle-weary soldier returning from the battlefield with nothing to justify what had happened. I wanted to run and hide—to wallow in my toxic shame. It was good of my parents to take me back into the family home. I will always be grateful for that.

I remember going straight to my bedroom and remaining in the darkness of my alcoholic mind for the rest of the night, replaying my whole life up to that point. I'm not sure if anyone came near me that evening. I suppose none of us knew what to do or how to cope with this dreadful situation. When I was at my neediest was when I hurt the most, as shame based families cannot support you. What I needed then was compassion, empathy, love, and support. I needed to be held by someone to stop me from falling apart. An alcoholic is someone who wants to be held while staying isolated. I just needed to know my family was on my side, even though I had screwed up badly. I needed a treatment centre or counselling at that time, but there was nothing available. Nobody knew what to do or how to help, so I am not blaming anyone, and I don't resent them. There was no training out there to prepare my family or me for this tragedy.

Three of my brothers and two of my sisters were still similar in age to Paul. *How must they feel*, I thought to myself but dare not ask anyone for fear it would cause a flood of my dammed up emotions, which I would not have been able to cope with at the time. It was best to not talk about the huge elephant in the room. The only way we all coped with it was by pretending everything was ok, that the accident never really happened. Small talk was the order of the day, as being alone with my alcoholic mind was an absolute living hell.

My personality had changed for the worst over the previous few days. I found it difficult to interact with people. I was always coming from a place of guilt and shame. I had retreated to the confines of my own mind: a dreary black hole of self-pity, guilt, shame, and victim mentality. Sadness lay all around waiting to trap me like quicksand. I lived beneath a clouded sky of depression and, while it was cold and morbid in there, it was a familiar place of retreat, where nobody but me could enter, and I could wallow alone. I had moved in, furnished this place, made it strangely comfortable, and lived in this place even before the accident happened. Years of alcoholism had turned my mind into a torture chamber. There was no spark left in me, no fun, no joy anymore; just depression, guilt, and self-pity. It felt like I'd died a few days earlier but was in limbo, buried under a mountain of guilt, shame, and remorse.

I didn't sleep much that first night at home. Thoughts ran riot in my head. *What if I had gone a different road? What if I had lost the keys and couldn't drive? What if I had given them to the barman? What if I was somewhere else? What if I just ended all? I wouldn't be a burden on my family anymore. Was it really my fault?* I questioned all the different options, hoping for an escape route from the guilt, but there was no escaping that I had caused Paul's death by driving while intoxicated. That was the truth of the matter. The more I tried to get away from them, the stronger they got. I had really screwed up this time. I had to try and accept that fact but I think I was still in shock because it seemed like it had happened to someone else.

As the faint morning light peeped through the curtains, much to my dismay, I had got through the second night. However, the battle of good and evil raged on inside my head. The sick gnawing feeling in the pit of my stomach was a clear indicator of who was winning. I looked across the room. My younger brothers lay sleeping. I thought of all the hurt and shame I had brought upon them and how much I loved them and wished I could have been a normal big brother to them. I just felt gutted. I thought of Paul and the Warren family. I immediately felt overwhelmed. The battle of self-defeating thoughts raged on now, and evil was winning all. I just lay there, hopeless and helpless, as silent rivers of emotions rolled freely down my cheeks and sneaked into my ears, filling them up, the pillow soaking up the rest of the liquid emotions.

It was about 6 am. I wanted to get up and get out of the torture chamber, yet I felt fear and had a morbid sense of security there. Also, I didn't want to wake the whole house up. I lay there for a while, tossing and turning in my little cocoon, annihilated by my crazy, shame-filled mind. Eventually, I got up and sneaked outside before anyone else arose. I felt scared, and I just wanted to run. I didn't know whether to turn right or left, as there was total confusion and chaos within me. If a car came down the road, I'd jump over the fence and hide, I felt so ashamed. I would try to lift myself up by promising I would never ever drink again. Despair, loneliness, self-pity, and guilt were my companions for the day. I walked down to the nearby shore, where it was quiet and lonely. I felt it was the only place I could hide away from everyone. I loved to hide away in sad and lonely places. That's where I spent the day wandering aimlessly and replaying my life. Glimpses of hope arose every now and then, as new scenarios about my life from there on played out like a merry dance, only to be engulfed by the black clouds of despair when the realisation of what happened hit. "If only" was a phrase constantly replaying in my mind. There was a lot of regret. I thought about diving into the water and letting it take me, but I lacked the courage needed to perform such an act, after trying to end it all the previous year.

Eventually, the day passed, and it felt like the longest day ever. Reluctantly, I returned home that evening. I was starving but felt unworthy of my parent's hospitality. I hated going back home, but I had nowhere else to go. Nobody else was talking to me, and I couldn't explain anything, not knowing how I felt. Besides, I didn't feel worthy of anyone's time. I knew I was responsible for Paul's death, yet I didn't set out to cause his death. It was a catch twenty-two situation. It was an unfortunate accident, but it was too enormous for me or my family to fully appreciate. I felt afraid and uncomfortable in my parent's home. They must have been so fed up of me making a mess of things. That was understandable, and there were awkward silences. You could cut the atmosphere with a knife.

If you made a mistake, it was your own fault and tough, get on with it. "You've made your bed, now lie on it" was a common saying when you screwed up. Although I had a great childhood in many ways, I felt home tended to be sad, serious, full of worry and fear. I was fortunate enough to have had great parents. We never wanted for anything and got the best possible opportunities regarding education. We were always well fed and taken care of. My parents did the best they could with what they knew. They always wanted the best for us. Yet, I always felt depressed and worthless as a child.

I hadn't eaten in two days, and there was thunder in my stomach, but I felt I didn't deserve to eat at my parents' table. I knew I had to get away before I cracked up. The crashed van was parked outside and every time I'd glance at it, I'd feel like something invisible would punch me in the gut. It was smashed up bad. Not that I needed one, but it was a savage reminder. I thought about the Warrens often and wanted to go tell them how sorry I was, but how could I go to them? How could I ever face them? How could I ever face anyone again? I felt they'd judge me, and what other people thought of me at the time was very important to me. However, I was the harshest judge of all. *Maybe it's best to crawl under the nearest rock*, I would think. My mother offered me some food, and I reluctantly ate something that evening then went back to the torture chamber.

After getting through the second night in my parent's house, I began to settle down a bit and realise there was nothing I could do to bring Paul back to life. So, the best option I could think of was to get away for a while. Where could I go? I had no money and nowhere I could go. Fear gripped me like a vice when I thought of the consequences. The next day, I had a visitor: Eleanor, a beautiful young girl from the town Paul came from. I didn't know her that well but had spoken to her in the pub on occasion. I believed God had sent one of his angels—what a pleasant surprise. She was only 16 at the time but was very kind and caring. It was the first piece of kindness and compassion shown to me since the accident. We talked and talked and tried to figure out what was the best course of action to take. Eventually, and reluctantly, she had to go home, so I walked her down the road a bit.

I felt a little better after she had called. I remember thinking, *I must not be that bad if someone actually called to see me.* She was the first person to call to see how I was, and she unknowingly saved my life that day. Eleanor held me that day and gave me unconditional love, which stopped me from falling apart, and I held on to that for a long time afterwards. I remember feeling so grateful to her, and I will always be. She is a wonderful person. I began to think of all the so-called friends I had in the pub. Only one of them called, but I wasn't that surprised. That was my great friend John, who called a few days later. He was the best buddy anyone could ask for. I believe he was another angel sent to me. I craved alcohol but tried to stay off it. I needed an anaesthetic, relief from the mental torture, as I was finding it increasingly difficult to cope with what had happened. I needed to escape from my own head, if only for a few hours. We went for a drive that day but I didn't drink.

The first few weeks passed and the reality of what happened was slowly sinking in. There were good days and bad days as time went by. I wanted to get away but was waiting for a summons for court. Then, finally the day came when the gardai called. It was the local gardai and they were okay with me. I was charged with dangerous driving, causing death, and careless driving. I'd expected that and was okay with it; even kind of relieved. They served the summons, and I had to show up in court two weeks later.

My friend John called every now and then, and we would go for a drive. One of the days John called, I asked him to take me to the Warren's house. I'd been thinking of going there for a while but didn't have the courage. I felt so guilty and remorseful. Remorse is closely linked to guilt. It is an emotional expression of regret felt after causing harm to another person. It's like the physical version of guilt that includes a strong desire to apologise to others. The decision was very difficult to make. While I wanted to go and say I was sorry for what happened, for causing Paul's death and injuring his brother Pat, I was also scared at how the family would take it. I didn't know if it was the right thing to do or if it was the right time. I didn't want to cause any more pain for them. I talked to John

drive drunk, walk sober

about it and decided this was something I must do. It was the least I could do, to try and make some sort of amends.

We set off for the Warren's house. It was a three-mile drive from my parent's house. It only took about fifteen minutes to get there, but there was a lot of indecision along the way. I asked John to turn back a few times but thankfully he kept going. *Am I doing the right thing by going there? Maybe I should just stay away. Why are you actually going? Is it to ease your own conscience or to help the Warrens?* I would ask myself. We finally arrived outside the Warren's house. It was a long bungalow up a steep hill. I was terrified but also knew this was something I had to do. I at least owed them this much. I asked the power within me to grant me the courage to get out of the car and walk up the hill. My heart was pounding, my stomach churning, and my body trembling. It took all my strength and courage to just get myself out of the car. I thought of turning back, but the voice inside said to keep going. I glanced back as I trudged the hill. John stayed in the car. I wished he had come with me. It felt like my feet were encased in concrete, every step laboured.

I knocked on the door. I felt absolutely gutted with shame, guilt, remorse, and every negative emotion that existed. I felt very vulnerable. I was trembling badly. I wanted to turn back and run down the hill again, but now it was too late. Paul's mother had opened the door. I burst out crying, head down in shame as I blurted out my name and she said she knew. She was crying also. She asked me to come in. I was shaking with fear. I'm not sure if anyone else was in the house at the time. We both broke down crying, and the atmosphere was powerful. I blurted out my apology, saying that I was very—very—sorry for what happened. She thanked me for coming and for my sincere apology. She was a very understanding woman. I don't think I'd be capable of the strength and compassion she showed me that day. I wanted to throw my arms around her and just hold her but thought, *No, it's probably not the right thing to do just now.* I definitely would not have been as understanding as that lady, if my child had been killed. I stayed for a little while and she talked about Paul and Pat and what they were like. It was just heart-breaking and very difficult to listen to, knowing that because of me Paul was no longer alive. It was a surreal experience. I wanted to bolt out the door at first, but now I was glad I had faced this. I thought, *How can that poor woman cope with the loss of her son? Oh, my God!* I couldn't let myself think too much about it, for fear of cracking up. Then, she gave me a memorial card with Paul's photo on it. I still have that little card today.

Then we said our goodbyes, and I left the house that day totally blown away by the kindness and compassion Paul's mother had shown me. I couldn't cope any longer. I was expecting to be shouted and screamed at, even hit with some blunt instrument; that might have made me feel a little better. I did feel a little better that I had gone there. I have never had to call on such strength and courage from within since that day. It takes massive courage to go to a parent when you have caused the death of their child. It's the hardest thing I've ever had to do in my life. I ran down the hill and I pleaded with John to take me to the pub, as I just became overwhelmed with grief and needed something to help me cope or escape the feelings. However, John didn't think it was a good idea, so we didn't go that day or the next day. I felt relieved I'd gone to see Paul's mother and said my piece. I also felt relieved I didn't go drinking.

drive drunk, walk sober

The court case was getting closer now. I didn't know what to expect and didn't care. I just wanted to be punished. John took me to court that morning, where the case was simply heard and adjourned to a higher court in the city for hearing, the following February. I knew then that I was going to get a prison sentence. This was August, and I would have to wait another eight months to discover my fate. I wished it to be over sooner. John guaranteed £10,000 bail for me, and I was released. He was a great friend then and still is today. Reality hit home with the realisation that I was going to get time in jail. On one hand, I wanted to be punished and thought it might ease the guilty feelings, but I also wanted to flee. I was scared but knew it was the least I could do to help the Warren and Walsh families now.

My mother suggested I go away to the UK until the court case came up. For the first time ever, I agreed with her. I knew my parents were destroyed at what I had done and disappointed at the way I had turned out, and I knew it was the best thing for everyone if I just got out of Ireland altogether, at least until the court case.

My old buddy John called that evening and we went to town. I was so delighted to be getting away from home again, but also craving alcohol just to escape from my own head for a while. I convinced John to take me to the bar and promised I'd only have one or two (famous last words). I genuinely believed that thought, just like every other time preceding alcohol. I thought maybe one drink might be okay. This was the usual thought, *Sure, one would do no harm.*

We went to the bar and I ordered a drink, which I remember vividly: vodka and Coke. I'd had no alcohol for about a month at this stage, so it hit my body with a bang, like the first time

The Night That Would Haunt Me

I tried whiskey in the marquee all those years ago. I almost immediately felt relief as I swallowed that one down. As usual, I had no control and promptly ordered another, and another, until before I knew it, I was drunk again. I was on the merry go round again. Then came the alcoholic guilt—I couldn't believe I had started drinking again after all that had happened. I had sworn to myself I would never ever drink again, and here I was pounding the bar, bewildered, saying "Why? Why?" It was just plain insanity.

After all the pep talks I had given myself and all the promises I had made to my family and myself, here I was again taking the poison to kill the pain. I had promised my family that I would never ever drink again and sincerely meant it, and yet here I was wanting no more alcohol, yet being powerless to stop it. I had no defence against even the first drink. I had to go home that evening, drunk only four weeks after the accident, and face my mother and father. My family couldn't believe it either … my mother was angry and my father remained silent as usual, but I could hear them arguing over me in the kitchen when I went to bed.

The next morning, my mother called my aunt Agnes in the UK, a kind and loving lady with a heart of gold. She was another angel, and agreed to take me into her home. Within a few days, I was on the ferry to England. It was best for everyone that I leave, now that I had started drinking again.

After around twenty hours of travelling, I arrived at the Oxford train station, sometime in early September of 1985. I hadn't shaved or eaten in a few days and looked like an escaped convict. But I recognised my dear aunt Agnes straight away, even though I hadn't seen her in fourteen years. She welcomed me and took me into her humble home. After a week there, I realised this situation was like jumping out of the frying pan and into the fire, but I was so tired and weary with literally nowhere else to go. All my bridges were burned at that stage.

Luckily, I managed to get a job within a few days and looked forward to the wages at the weekend. Here I could carry on drinking and nobody really cared. I remember falling into a stream one day, drunk as usual and I couldn't climb out of it. Everyone just walked past as if I was invisible, I was sat in it for ages before I managed to crawl out of it. My aunt remained silent, as this was normal behaviour in her home. I drank my way through those eight months in the UK and couldn't cope without it. Alcohol, along with causing my problems, had also become my anaesthetic. It destroyed my life, then stopped me from going crazy and ending it all. It had me under complete control. Depression, loneliness, self-pity, guilt, shame, and despair were my constant companions. I felt completely isolated, exiled from my native land. England felt like a cold and harsh country, where the people were different, and the culture was different. I couldn't relate properly due to the toxic shame I unknowingly carried around within me.

I thought about what had happened often, about Paul and his family, and the Walshes, and then I'd become overwhelmed with guilt and go straight to the bar. How must they have felt? It was a dark and desperate time, devoid of hope. My confidence was practically gone, and I found it difficult to make friends, as I felt less than everyone and unworthy of companionship. I thought if people really knew what I had done they wouldn't want anything to do with me. Suicide was on my mind a lot but the crazy thing was, alcohol stopped me from doing that by numbing the pain it had caused. I got paid on a Friday and by Monday, all my money was gone on alcohol. This continued while I was there, although every Monday I'd promise myself next Friday I wouldn't go drinking, and save some money instead. But as soon as Friday evening came I was off to the pub again. I desperately needed the anaesthetic. I no longer cared what anyone thought of me and was always insanely drunk at the weekends. Thankfully, my dear aunt somehow tolerated my behaviour, as I was her brother's son and she idolised my father. Otherwise, I would have been completely lost in a haze of alcohol, guilt, and self-pity.

The day of reckoning was fast approaching now, and I would soon have to go home and face the consequences of my drinking. I still wanted it over and done with but was scared and wanted to run. I had a feeling I was going to get a while in prison. Deep down, I didn't care what happened to me anymore. My insides were like a barren wasteland.

I arrived home a few days before court. The atmosphere was much the same as the last time, and I could understand why. On the morning of the court case, I silently got dressed in the old grey suit I had bought six years previously for a neighbour's wedding. I quietly left the house that morning. There were no goodbyes or good luck wishes. My family didn't know how to cope with this tragedy, so it was basically me and my best buddy John. I had to walk to my local town that morning, as John was working and couldn't pick me up from home. I couldn't ask my dear father for a lift, I felt so ashamed. The cold wind cut through my threadbare grey suit that morning, as I walked the long road to the town and towards my fate.

No words could describe the emptiness and hopelessness I felt that morning. These feelings were familiar now. They were my constant companions. I didn't care if I lived or died anymore. As far as I was concerned, I had died on that awful night of the accident. I felt alienated from the human race. Home was no longer home, and it had just become a place to get my head down and hide these days. There was no communication or affection available there, with no one capable of talking about the elephant in the room.

As I walked up the long, windy road to the town, little faces with beady eyes and pointed noses peeped out from behind twitching lace curtains. I felt angry at the neighbours: the people I grew up with in the village, the men that gave me drops of beer out of their bottles and laughed. But now not even one of them called to see how my parents or I were doing. We were supposed to be a small, close knit community, or so I thought. I had grown up with these people and yet there was no support from any of them. I suppose I expected something off them but later discovered that expectations are the makings of resentments. It reminded me of the twilight zone. The road was lined with judges and juries, sitting in their comfortable ruts. No heroic cheers or flowers lined the roads for me. I was judging the judges. I had become the greatest judge of all, and I resented them all, and I resented myself. The battle of good and evil raged on inside as I walked the road of my destiny.

I wanted punishment, in the hope that I could let this go and move on with my life. I was frightened, but I felt this was the only tangible act I could do now to try and ease the pain of the Warrens and Walshes. I wanted at least five years in jail. My life was destroyed anyway, so it didn't matter. Suddenly, I could hear a blackbird singing in the whitethorn hedge as I walked along. It immediately transported me back to my childhood days and the great times spent with my father on the farm. They were such blissful days hanging out with my hero. I felt very sad and thought, *If only I could go back in time, things would be so different.* I was always living in the past or the future. Never in the present moment.

After walking for an hour, I finally got to the town and met John. He drove us to the city, and we met the barrister in a hotel next to the court. He was very professional. There were ongoing discussions about the best possible outcome. It was agreed I would plead guilty, as I knew I was the cause of Paul's death, and I desperately wanted to show the Warrens that I was sorry for what I had done.

We then left for the court, and as I was coming near the court, I stumbled upon Paul's father. My heart started pounding, and I felt overwhelmed with fear, shame, and guilt. I had not seen him since the accident happened. He was walking up the steps of the courtroom and I ran alongside him, and I apologised to him as best I could as we walked up the steps to the courtroom, and I remember him saying, "We'll have to try and get on with our lives as best we can after this." If it was my son that had died, I don't know if I would have been as polite to the person that caused his death. I think I would have kicked him up and down the steps a few times.

Going into the court, I felt frozen with fear but was also relieved it had come to this day, as the court and the consequences were constantly on my mind. I just wanted it over with, once and for all. I felt that the whole world was against me, and only my buddy John was there on my side. Then, I saw my two sisters in the courtroom. It was heart-warming to see two friendly faces out there, and it thawed me out a little. It was great to see some support from my family there, although it could not have been easy for them to deal with. I am forever grateful to them for showing up, and it meant the world to me.

The courtroom was full of people at the back and solicitors and gardai at the front. The judge naturally had the highest bench looking down on everyone. I sat at the back with my sisters and John, waiting for my case to be called. Eventually my case was called, I was called to the stand. My heart was pounding so loudly that I wondered if anyone else could hear it. The charges were read out, and I was asked how I pleaded. "Guilty," I shakily replied. Not once did it occur to me to plead any other way, as I valued life, honesty, and truth. I didn't want to put anyone involved through any more suffering. It was over in minutes. I was sentenced to twelve months in prison and a five-year ban from driving. While I felt that I should have gotten more punishment, I was somewhat relieved that I didn't. Once it was all over, I was allowed to speak to my sisters and John before the gardai escorted me to a cell in the local garda station. My belt and tie were taken from me as a precaution.

My emotions went from one extreme to the other: relief to despair. I thought, *This is not the answer to what had happened to Paul. I need counselling or something.* I cried and cried like a baby in the cell. I was locked up in a prison cell for a crime I committed as a result of my disease. My freedom had been taken away from me, leading me to panic in the cell. I'd never been locked up in a confined space before, and there was nowhere I could run to. It was suffocating and I trembled with fear, trapped like a rat in a cage.

Finally, it hit home that this was it for the next twelve months, and my whole life flashed before me. I came to the realisation, this was where alcohol had finally brought me. The time seemed to drag on in that cell. As I counted the minutes, they felt like hours. The Gardai told me that I would be taken to

Mount joy Prison in Dublin later that day. I thought about Paul and all that happened in the previous nine months because of alcoholism. I swore off alcohol again, in my prison cell. My whole life up until that day was replaying in front of my eyes. All the damage I had caused in the last ten years of drinking was very clear to me. I was twenty-five years old and the destruction of people and material things was all I had achieved. Had I never picked up alcohol, my life would have been a lot different.

I built my hopes up by confirming to myself, *Never again am I putting a drop of alcohol to my lips. This is a new beginning. I'll die first before I drink again.* This was the post drinking mantra I had used many times before, after fallout from drinking. It gave me a hopeful boost I needed. Little did I realise, I'd be drunk again before the day was over.

Chapter 2

Consequences

Keys rattled in the lock of the prison cell door. I jumped up, knots in my stomach from fear and anticipation. It slowly creaked open, and in came two prison officers and a detective. For the first time ever, I was handcuffed. They felt strangely heavy in comparison to the ones we played with as children, and were tight on my wrists, confirming my legitimacy as a criminal. I thought, *Is there any need for these? Am I that dangerous?* "It's only a precaution," they said. "Standard procedure." It was a weird feeling, being handcuffed. I remember wondering what my father would have thought if he'd seen me then.

"We'll take them off you when we get onto the bus," the officer explained. They were true to their word. It was around 4 pm when we left the garda station with all four of us in this minibus, heading for Dublin 150 miles away, which was usually a four-hour drive. The officers were kind and friendly towards me. They didn't think anyone was going to prison that day, and they'd planned a drinking session for themselves on the way back. I told them that I didn't mind what they did, that they could handcuff me to the seat and go off to the bar

drive drunk, walk sober

and I'd stay put. After all, I came back from England for the trial. I just didn't care what they did. "No, no, you're coming with us," they said. Well, I couldn't believe it.

There I was after getting a twelve-month prison sentence, going out drinking with the detective and two prison officers. How ironic. I couldn't believe what was happening. I thought all my Christmases had come at once. After driving for an hour, we stopped at a bar and had a few pints in there. It felt surreal. I was delighted and felt more at ease after getting some alcohol down me. The earlier promise I had made to myself never to drink again was already a distant memory. That was what usually happened. I had absolutely no willpower when it came to alcohol.

After two drinks there, we moved on to another town. I had attended boarding school there ten years earlier. I wondered if Mountjoy jail could be as tough as that place. We had many more drinks there, and I found myself getting drunk already, as I could not tolerate much alcohol. We left there and our last stop was in Longford. We stayed in that pub until closing time and were all a bit merry at this stage.

While in Longford, the thought crossed my mind to phone home. With no mobile phones back then, I went to a payphone down the street. I could have run at any time, but what would have been the point? I phoned home and spoke to my father. He couldn't understand how I was drunk and ringing home from halfway across the country, when I was supposed to be in jail. I explained to him what was going on. He didn't know what to think. I went back to the bar after that and had many more beers. I couldn't believe what was happening. The three men who were supposed to be escorting me to prison were now fairly well drunk. Nobody could drive safely, so one of the officers drove the bus out of town to the nearest layby, where we all fell asleep. We must have been asleep for hours. Eventually, I awoke craving more alcohol and could see the three officers sprawled out on the seats.

Eventually everyone woke up, and we continued our journey to Dublin, which was about another hour and a half. My stomach was churning when we arrived outside the gates of Mountjoy jail. It was in the middle of the night, around 4 am I think. The officers were on a walkie talkie, trying to contact the prison. There was no answer, so we were locked out of jail. It was funny at the time. I couldn't believe it and never imagined this would happen. Everyone was hungover and the mood was not good. All four of us were stuck inside a bus for at least two more hours, hungover and moody. The welcomed dawn arrived eventually, and the little walkie talkie crackled, followed by the sound of the prison officer inside. The officers warned me not to say a word about this, to which I agreed, and they would make sure I was looked after inside. I was very grateful for the last drink on the way up and kept my mouth firmly closed, but felt the usual post drinking guilt. I had broken the promise to myself to never drink again.

The big, black double doors opened slowly, and I was taken inside Mountjoy jail, to a reception area. All doors were locked, bars were on all windows, and there were even bars on the tiny windows in the doors. I thought, *Are they trying to reinforce the fact we're in jail?* Reality was hitting home. My freedom was gone now; my life not my own anymore. I was told to strip off and given prison clothes, with my old, grey suit confiscated. I was presented with a wine jumper and trousers, a shirt vest, underpants, socks, and black shoes, all recycled and handed down from some other unfortunate soul.

drive drunk, walk sober

I was searched, went in for a shower, got dressed, was finger printed, and had my photo taken holding up a board in front of my chest with a number on it. It was all very mechanical.

I was only a number now, with a criminal record. This was upsetting but also the consequence of drinking and driving, and taking Paul's life. I had to stay strong now and get through this, thanks to the amazing resilience I had and always had. I was given breakfast then, which resembled something I would not even feed to the dog. Still sick from the drink the night before, I wasn't in the humour for eating prison food.

After eating, I was taken to my cell, which consisted of bunk beds, two lockers, and two piss pots. The brick walls were painted white, covered in posters of semi-naked ladies and the lino-like substance on the floor was highly polished. It looked cosy and inviting. The door was small and looked solid; no danger of kicking that open. I was introduced to my cell mate. He kindly informed me that I was sleeping on the bottom bunk. The door clunked into place and that was it. I was locked away with some stranger, both of us having to piss or shit into a pot if the urge came upon us. Somehow, I felt safe in there, although I panicked at times, when I realise I couldn't get out.

The time ticked away very slowly. The other prisoner asked what I was in for, so I told him and asked him what he was in for. He was doing twelve years for armed robbery. We got on okay, and he filled me in on what to do and what not to do. Within a few weeks, I became acclimatised to the place. The only thing I really missed was my freedom, yet there was a sense of security in there. I had plenty of time to reflect on all that had happened in the last few years, and to wonder how my family was and what they were doing. It felt so weird to be

Consequences

alive yet have no freedom, even to go to the toilet when you wanted.

Somehow, I didn't feel I belonged in there. My life was destroyed but what else could I do? What else could the government do to cater for victims of these types of accidents? I had to accept this was going to be my home for the next twelve months. I thought it might ease the guilt and shame I had over what had happened, but sadly it didn't. We were locked in the cell for twenty-two hours a day. I was not a great talker, I preferred to stay within the confines of my own mind. We had two hours to walk around the yard or go to the library. It was not easy, and the time passed very slowly. They let us out in the morning to empty our piss pots, or slop out as it was called, then we had breakfast. We had a shower twice a week and could wash every morning. There were the usual bullies and gangs in there, but I just kept my head down and minded my own business like my cell mate had advised. Birds of a feather flock together, but I hadn't met anyone else who was in for what I was in for. I was a loner anyway and stuck to myself most of the time. The prison had a library where I could get books every day. Thank God for that, as I loved reading and that helped pass the hours away.

It often occurred to me that I could have done something of use as punishment, besides this prison sentence; maybe something useful for someone as repayment. However, I hoped it gave some sort of relief to the Warren family. Was it the right punishment for the crime I had committed? Maybe a mandatory addiction treatment programme, even after the first time I was caught drinking and driving, might have prevented this. I thought, if I wasn't drinking, I would have been driving normally. Alcoholic drinking had caused

Paul's death, and unfortunately, I was the alcoholic behind the wheel that evening. I had plenty of time to reflect on my life. At twenty-five years of age, it felt like my life was already over.

I spent about a month in Mountjoy Prison, or "the joy" as it was lovingly called. Losing my freedom to choose what to do for the day was a big blow to me, as I was used to doing my own thing. I was very strong willed. One morning, I was called into the governor's office. I was told, "You are being transferred to Loughan house, in county Cavan today." I didn't know what that place was but no longer had a choice in where I went. About six of us were put on a minibus and transferred to this open prison. My closed mouth had paid off. After about two hours' travelling, we arrived at what looked like a large school. There were guys walking around the grounds, and only the uniforms would give away that it was a prison.

It was an open prison, where we weren't locked up in cells anymore, but I had my own prison cell within my own head. I shared a room with some guy from Monaghan. We got on fine. It was a good place and I liked it. We could go to school and improve ourselves, and also do crafts and woodwork. I made some beautiful marquetry pieces and made furniture for some of my family, as a way of trying to make amends. I also made furniture for some other inmates, specialising in making baby chairs. I was allowed to sell them and the money was put in an account in the prison. I was making money whilst inside. The days passed and the nights were long, but we played poker for ounces of tobacco. There was plenty of cannabis around as well, so being stoned helped cope with the loss of my freedom. I was happy enough there although my nickname was depression. John and Eleanor visited every weekend and so did my two sisters. I was very grateful for their support. The time passed more quickly than it had at the Joy, and I was due to get out on temporary release at Christmas. I didn't want to go but was told I had to go.

I had become institutionalised, but I was released despite objections and went straight to the bar. I was drunk that night and for the whole week I was out. Nothing had changed in me, except I had withdrawn more and more into myself. I no longer felt good enough to socialise with others. I didn't feel liked or worthy even before the accident, I thought most people hated and judged me. After Christmas, I was glad to go back to jail, where I felt safe and secure. The next two months passed quickly, and I was due for release. Again, I didn't want to go but had to. I was being thrown out of jail—how could they? Ha ha! I was released after ten months.

It was scary facing the real world again with a head full of guilt, remorse, and toxic shame. The time in prison didn't ease the guilt like I thought it would. I had put all those feelings on hold while inside, but now I was at large again. What would I do? Where would I go? Where could I get a job around my local town after what happened, especially after being banned off the road for another four years?. There was no support anywhere. I was basically on my own now. How could I face the Warrens or Walshes ever again? The best thing I could do was to go back to England, out of the way. I had made over £700 in prison, so now I had plenty of money in my pocket. I decided I'd have one more drink before going away. I promised myself I'd stop drinking for good and start a new life in England.

Chapter 3

On the Run

Her long, claw-like nails glided the cards out onto the green felt cloth with ultimate precision. She was blonde and good looking, her red lipstick impeccably applied to perfectly shaped lips, and her sparkling blue eyes dazzled me, as she smiled and beckoned me over to the blackjack table. I was like a moth to the flame. Getting attention from a beautiful woman after the way I was feeling just boosted my ego. I was mesmerised by the attention. I'd been released from prison after serving my time for dangerous driving causing death. I'd been set free to make a new life for myself. I drank for two days straight and then finally made the ferry to England. My eyes were blurry and distorted due to the alcoholic anaesthetic, my relief from the pain of reality.

I'd saved £700 in the prison by making furniture for the inmates. Now, in a haze of alcohol, I was going to make fifty times that much at the blackjack table. *I'm a professional gambler, an expert at this game,* I thought. I was in full flight from reality, the drink was flowing, the cards were gliding, and my money was sliding away from me into the blonde's pockets. Before I knew it, we had arrived at Holyhead in Wales and I was penniless again, after all my hard work and saving. In my drunken state, I had gambled absolutely everything and lost. This was familiar territory. I didn't even have the price of a train ticket to my aunt's house. I was ruined again all because I had picked up that first drink. It was a poor start to my new life in England.

How did that happen after all the trouble I was in? I'd give myself the usually telling off and then promise myself this would never happen again. The lack of control used to drive me crazy with guilt. I knew the drink had me by the neck, but I couldn't survive without it. My life had revolved around alcohol for the past nine years.

It was the only solution I knew of for the toxic shame I felt inside. My whole past came rushing back to me again like it usually did when I was down and out. The little boy in me cried out for his daddy, but there was no daddy anymore. It always came down to daddy when I was in trouble. It was like I never really progressed from that stage of childhood. If I was to survive this self-imposed exile in this cold, foreign land, then I'd have to get sober and recover. Looking back now, I was in no fit state, mentally, to go back to England. A treatment centre would have been a far better option, but I was in denial and so was everyone else that had anything to do with me. They just wanted rid of me, and I wanted to run away as far as possible.

I thought about jumping out in front of a moving train, because that would finish it once and for all, but I didn't have the strength to end it. What was I to do? I had hit another rock bottom. Here I was in a foreign country with not even the price of a box of matches in my pocket. Panic set in, I was scared but pride wouldn't let me call home for help. I couldn't do that anymore, so reluctantly I called my dear aunt and told her I was robbed on the ferry, which was not far from the truth. I asked her If she wouldn't mind paying for the train ticket, and I would pay her back as soon as I got working again. The stress of having to go through that situation was so severe, I wonder how I kept going at all. I know I had inner strength that I seemed to rely upon when the chips were down.

My aunt said yes like she always did, as she was a beautiful soul, and I took the train back to her house. I thank God she was in my life, as I had absolutely nobody else to turn to. She was an angel and I'm eternally grateful for her in my life. Little did I realise then, my life was not going to change for the better for the next eight years, with a head full of guilt and a belly full of toxic shame. I dulled the pain of living with alcohol. I had sunk deeper and deeper into depression isolation and despair. I had lost all confidence and respect in myself. After a while living in the UK, I met a local girl and we moved in together. I was in no fit state for a relationship. I felt unworthy of love or anyone's attention, and that blocked me from any meaningful relationship. However, we managed to have two beautiful daughters. I was incapable of being emotionally or physically available for those girls until after I got sober. That relationship was very dysfunctional, and eventually it came to an end. I was thrown out, as that's what usually happens alcoholics, and I had to find another place to live.

I also acquired a new driving licence in England and was hanging in workwise, but I continued to drink and drive, and eventually got caught three times in two months, thankfully before any accident occurred and got banned for five years with a two-month prison sentence. I was used to prison, so I fooled myself into thinking that it didn't bother me, even though I had a constant knot in my stomach with fear. I had become very hardened.

However, after years of hard work in the construction industry, I injured my back and had to take time off work. I had no money saved up as usual, so I got thrown out of my accommodation as I couldn't pay the rent and had nowhere else to live. I couldn't ask my dear aunt to take me in again; it wouldn't have been fair. God knows she had enough to deal with, so I ended up sleeping rough in the local park.

Sleeping on park benches at night and eating out of dustbins was where I had arrived after six years working hard in the UK. This was where I had arrived because of alcohol, at thirty-one years of age—homeless and completely broken. Thank God it was around early summer and the weather was warm. There was a sense of freedom in it though. There was no rent to pay, no electricity bills, and no responsibility, which is what I always wanted all my life. I felt free and didn't care what happened to me or what anyone thought of me most of the time, yet this powerful voice within me subtly reminded me I could do better. Alcohol had become my master, first by making me suffer and then easing my pain all at once giving me a false sense of security. I realised I was finished in England. I was burned out. I had to get back to Ireland if I had any chance of survival. Pride wouldn't let me go back to my dear aunt, who must have been sick of me hanging around and not being able to move on. I knew I was due a tax rebate, so that was the only hope I had of getting home again.

I thought of Paul, his brother, and the driver often and bashed myself with the guilty club. I thought of my family and my dad and toxic shame would rise up in me. I was scared to think too much about what had happened to the Warrens, the Walshes, and my own family. As soon as I'd allow myself to think about what happened, I would become overwhelmed and have to change the thoughts, as I was afraid of losing my sanity. I couldn't cope with the reality of the situation at all. There was no let up.

Finally, the tax rebate cheque arrived at my aunt's house. I was never as delighted to receive a cheque as that day. The first thing I did was buy a ticket home. I then spent two days drinking and Dean, my only real friend in England, drove me to the airport. I vaguely remember thinking I wouldn't be back. I had failed miserably at trying to live normally with the guilt and pain I carried. I just wasn't able to function. I needed help in the worst way. I was beaten physically and mentally. I don't remember the flight that day, but I was relieved at coming home. Maybe I could find the help, love, and care I needed back in my native land.

My brother picked me up from the airport. I was the worse for wear when I arrived with my small suitcase packed with a few old clothes and a pair of working boots. I was ten stone in weight, and my self-esteem read zero. Looking back, I was never going to forgive myself for causing Paul's death. I'd hardly talked to anyone about the accident during those eight years in England. Very few people knew the real me back there.

When I arrived home, my family welcomed me. My mother said I could stay at home and help my younger brother on the farm. I had become cold and isolated. I was like a block of ice. I stayed at home for about a month or two, getting my dole money every week and having one day of drinking a week. My mother and some of my siblings were not impressed with my lifestyle. I knew I had to get out of home sooner than later.

drive drunk, walk sober

I had become totally selfish and self-centred. I was incapable of showing compassion for anyone. I was in survival mode. All I wanted to do was get drunk, to escape this reality, the accident, and it was in my head constantly.

While in town one day, I met an old school buddy of mine who had been going through rough times, and I decided to move into the doss house he was living in. There were three other alcoholics surviving in there. We were drunk and stoned most of the time, it was an alcoholic's paradise; complete escapism when we could afford it but highly depressing when all of us were broke. A lot of the time, I didn't know what day of the week or time of day it was. I remember going into town at five or six in the morning and thinking it was evening, looking for booze, wondering why everywhere was closed. Then, I'd realise it was morning, not evening. It seemed like a great setup at the time, but now I realise it was the end of the road for me. This powerful voice within me was saying, "Hey, Sean, this life is not for you. You can do better. You must pull yourself out of this." That motivated me and gave me the strength and courage to start looking for work and try and get my life back on track.

I got a job with a local construction firm. It was poorly paid, but it was a step in the right direction. I hated it though and just wanted to be back in the doss house getting drunk with the rest of the boys. I no longer wanted to work. Within three months, I lost that job due to missing days.

chapter 4

The Serial Drunk Driver

Then, I became friendly with a local taxi driver and we became drinking buddies, and I managed to convince him to give me a job driving his taxi. I managed to get a new, clean driving licence here in Ireland by exchanging my already banned UK licence. And just like that, I was back on the road once again. I started to drink and drive again, it was as if nothing ever happened. When I'd sober up, I used to feel really scared and angry at myself that I had driven while intoxicated after all that had happened ten years previous.

I was driving drunk, taking the people home who wouldn't drink and drive themselves. I ended up in a few brawls here and there. Then, I moved to another taxi company and was driving a school bus part-time. Sometimes, I would go to the pub with the intention of having one drink after the school run in the morning, and end up drinking all day and then driving a bus load of children home from school in the evening. When I'd sober up, I'd think, "Oh, my God, how can you do this after what happened, you must be crazy in the head, what the hell is wrong with you?" and then the promise of, "I'll never drink and drive again," would come. However, as soon as I'd pick up

drive drunk, walk sober

a drink, I'd be driving again. A vehicle in the hands of a drunk driver is a lethal weapon. I was out of control. I knew if I didn't put a stop to this, some other disaster was going to happen. I hated being like that, but as soon as I picked up a drink, I was incapable of any proper sense or reasoning. I was incapable of making a sane decision, my mind was not sound, whenever I drank alcohol.

Since the accident almost thirty-two years ago, I have asked myself thousands of times, *What if I'd made a different decision that night?* But there were no sane decisions once I picked up alcohol. As far as I can figure out, I just did the next thing that came into my head. What about the decision to get behind the wheel that night? I know before I went to the pub I had planned to go home at some point and collect Mary's going away present. I had decided on that before I even went to the bar. The plan was to go in and just have one, then go home for the present. However, as soon as I had that one drink, any sense or reason or choices no longer existed. What if I'd had the common sense to give the keys of the van to someone? There is no such thing as common sense when it comes to the disease of alcoholism. Did I ever have the sanity to hand over the keys to anyone? No, never, unless someone took them off me after a fight or argument, which was rare enough. I was always convinced in my own head, I was sober and okay to drive. What if the van had failed to start? I have wished that since the accident. How different life would have been for everyone involved.

Ordinary social drinkers will probably not understand this. Explaining alcoholism to a normal drinker is like trying to explain a colour to a blind person. Who can understand drunk driving? Only drunk drivers will understand, that even they cannot understand it. It's just baffling. I cannot understand it after all that's happened.

The first bad experience with drunk driving I can remember, was driving to a disco one night. I was driving up town with my sister in the car, drunk as usual even though I was convinced I was okay to drive. I stopped abruptly and another car crashed into the back of me. Normally, the person who rear-ended you would be at fault, but I was drunk and accepted liability. The damage was minimal, but I was drunk and incapable of driving safely. That was the first warning I didn't listen to. It would have been a deterrent to a normal drinker, but not an alcoholic.

Six months later, I crashed that same car into a river on Christmas Eve, writing it off. Thankfully, nobody else was involved and I had no injuries. I had been drinking all night but was not convinced I was drunk. That was a second warning I didn't listen to. Still, I didn't learn anything from that experience.

Eight months later, I was driving home from a night out, mounted a footpath and knocked a girl down. She was not seriously injured, but this was serious and could have been a lot worse. Yet, I still didn't learn anything from it. I was really scared the next morning, when I realised what had happened and promised I would never drink and drive again. However, I was drinking and driving a week later. That was my third warning, but I still didn't learn.

I continued to drink and drive. It was insanity. Three years later, I got arrested for drunk driving and got banned for eighteen months; still didn't learn anything.

drive drunk, walk sober

Six months after getting back on the road, I drove drunk again and caused the death of Paul.

Now, you would think any sane person who caused that much damage would definitely never drink again, never mind drinking and driving. However, it still did not fully register with me that I had a problem with alcohol. Presently, I accept my mind is not sound when it comes to alcohol. Until I got treatment, my thinking was strangely insane concerning anything to do with alcohol, yet it seem to be okay when it involved any other area of my life.

I acquired a new driving licence when I moved to England. I continued to drink and drive. After a short period of driving, I was arrested within three months for drunk driving. I was arrested three times in two months, but thankfully there was no accident this time. I got banned for five years and two months in prison, but I still did not learn.

Why was I convinced I was okay to drive when the reality was, I was incapable of driving? What could I have done? The only conclusion I can arrive at, is my judgement was impaired when drinking and the danger of drinking and driving seemed minimised.

Now, eight years later, I was driving a taxi and a school bus while drunk, and I still did not learn anything. I continued to drink and drive as if nothing had happened. Finally, I had another accident and hit some cows early in the morning, on my way to pick up children for school while still under the influence of alcohol. Maybe this particular morning, still intoxicated from the night before yet hazily aware of my senses, I think I was capable of making the sane decision not to drive. But I made the decision to drive, as I was on my final warning from the owner of the bus. I just sat behind the wheel and drove like I usually did the morning after. This was the first time I realised I was not fit for driving, and that was due to the fact I had around four hours sleep since my last drink. Basically, I was prepared to risk children's lives for alcohol. That was the reality. I thought of nothing else but alcohol, directly or indirectly, since I first picked it up as a teenager. I was obsessed and possessed with it. It was the only way I knew of to escape the horrible worthless feelings I had.

So, what about all the other drunk driving incidences?

Did I ever say to myself, "This is not a good idea, you're drunk and incapable of driving?" No.

Did I remember any of the previous incidents before I got behind the wheel? Maybe vaguely, but my mind would be blurry and the seriousness of the last situation minimised, as well as the promise that next time would be different.

Did I remember having a sane conversation with myself, saying things like, "This is not a wise or safe thing to do"? No, definitely not.

Am I capable of driving? YES.

Am I a danger to other road users? NO.

I was incapable of making a sane decision about driving, yet I was capable of making a decision to travel from one location to another. How was I able to make that decision and not the right one about driving? The only conclusion I can arrive at is, my mind put little emphasis on how to get from A to B. I had pre-planned to go and get the present for Mary and not given sufficient thought to how I would get there. Therefore, blindly,

drive drunk, walk sober

I focused on getting there rather than how to get there. Maybe the potential reward of giving the present cancelled out my realisation of the danger. I think decisions that would gratify the childlike selfishness within me over ruled any others.

When it involved driving, I think my mind was in denial of the danger involved. It was incapable of recognising the danger of drunk driving. I had driven impaired many times before so my mind must have registered drunk driving as being acceptable.

But what about the first accident, the rest of the accidents, and paul's death?

Did these events not register in my mind?

I think they vaguely registered, but my mind was insane, and there wasn't sufficient importance attached to them.

I still don't have all the answers. I honestly don't know. I'm absolutely baffled by this. I think my mind was insane preceding the first drink, and then alcohol just took over, then dimmed my reasoning, so as to minimise the danger and approve of getting behind the wheel. Before I went to the bar, it did not even occur to me to organise an alternative means of transport home. In my mind, drunk driving was acceptable even after all the previous accidents. This was normal behaviour to me. There was a sense of entitlement to perpetually drive over the limit. I was convinced I was fine.

How do I explain that to a non-alcoholic person? Is it possible to make normal social drinkers understand something as baffling as the disease of alcoholism? Why was my mind incapable of highlighting the danger, even after Paul's death? Why was I still capable of drunk driving? Why was I incapable of recalling his death before getting behind the wheel with alcohol consumed? These were questions I asked myself for years, to which I have no answers, except to admit my judgement was impaired and my thinking was not sound when drinking and especially preceding the first drink.

When dealing with ordinary life issues, I seem to be as normal as the next person, but when it comes to alcohol I am strangely insane. My mind is definitely not sound when it comes to anything to do with alcohol. That is the only answer I can come up with for repeatedly drunk driving, even after Paul's death.

According to research carried out by the National Public Services Research Institute, "One of the chief influences upon the decision to drive impaired was simply a person's failure to recognise or admit that they were under the influence of alcohol."

Also, according to the National Institute on Alcohol Abuse and Alcoholism, "Kids and teens who get involved with alcohol at a young age are seven times more likely to be involved in an alcohol-related crash in their lives."

I am under no illusion that if I pick up alcohol again, I would drive while drunk. That is the serious nature of alcoholism. It just possesses my mind and I have no control.

Chapter 5

The Seed Had Been Planted

The most profound recollection I have of drinking alcohol was when I was about seven or eight years of age. Back then, in the 60s, most small farms in the west of Ireland planted crops of oats and barley as fodder for the animals, to help them through the long, dark winters. In the autumn, the crops were harvested, tied into sheafs, and built into round stacks in a small area on the farm called a haggard, which was surrounded by trees for shelter from the prevailing west winds. This was a busy area on the farm; a hive of activity in the late autumn, as cocks of hay and stacks of oats and barley were stored there. It was where all the fodder was stored for the winter. When the stacks of oats and barley were thrashed, the straw was used as bedding for animals, and the grain was used as valuable feed.

In October, the threshing machine weaved its way down the narrow, hawthorn hedged windy roads. It went from village to village to thrash these crops, followed by its entourage of joyful men wearing big black wellingtons, and armed with well-worn pitchforks on their shoulders. Many songs have been written about this annual event. The news of the thresher

drive drunk, walk sober

arriving spread far and near. Its arrival was the highlight of the year for a small country boy like me. All the men of the village teamed up and travelled from farm to farm, to help each other with the threshing. This was called a meitheal and was common practice back then.

This was an amazing machine, or mill, as some people called it. It was imposing to me as a seven-year old boy, with lots of belts and wheels protruding from its sides. I was fascinated with this big, beautiful machine. It was powered by a large belt connected to a tractor. It made a humming noise that could be heard for miles when in operation. The sound of the thresher and the sweet, encompassing laughter and loud voices of the men was music to my ears. I just loved the atmosphere and felt a sense of belonging. How it operated, was the sheafs of oats or barley were fed into the hopper at the top of the thresher, and the grain was separated from the straw, within this great machine. The man on the top feeding the sheafs into the hopper had the most dangerous job of all. There were no safety regulations back then. I know of one man who unfortunately lost his arm in an accident involving the hopper. Thankfully, I never witnessed such an ordeal.

At gatherings like this, crates of beer and bottles of poteen were freely available for the men. Poteen is an illegal whiskey, home distilled from barley or potatoes. It was distilled on many remote farms and was very powerful alcohol. It was a magical cure all and used in most homes as a medicine, as well as a social lubricant. When we were sick, my father made punch for us to drink, which was poteen, hot water, and sugar. I don't ever recall liking the taste or smell of it, but I loved the warm, electric feeling it gave me. Animals were also given poteen for many ailments. Poteen was seeped in Irish tradition and culture. It was called "uisce beatha," which means water of life.

However, the Phoenix beer was my favourite drink. It had a tangy, cutting taste with a slight kickback. I remember that on threshing days, it was normal for me to partake in drinking the dregs from the bottom of bottles, thoughtfully left behind by the well-meaning men. I loved the taste of it then but most importantly, the feeling of belonging it gave me, and I just couldn't get enough. I can remember the taste in my mouth, the smell of it. It's still as clear as the first day I ever tasted it.

There were ominous warnings from my mother back then. "Don't drink out of those bottles, there are snails in them." Maybe she spotted something in me back then. I don't know, but one thing was for sure: it didn't bother me whether there were snails in those bottles or not. There could've been crocodiles in them for all I cared. I was still drinking them and that was that, much to the amusement of the men. I had a very determined character and strong stubborn streak in me. I don't think I ever got drunk at that stage, but I remember feeling a little dizzy.

I felt part of the gang of men, like I belonged. It was the most wonderful feeling, and I think I associated that with drinking alcohol. I can still remember the humming sound of the threshing machine, the laughter and chat of the men, the smell of cigarette smoke, the smell of the freshly threshed straw, the smell and taste of the phoenix ale, and the beautiful, calm, almost magical atmosphere on those October evenings. The stage was set, the alcoholism seed planted, and now all it had to do was germinate and grow under the right conditions.

I have never experienced that feeling with the same intensity since and have travelled far and wide chasing it. That was the most enchanting time, and I felt I belonged on this earth. I think I associated belonging with drinking alcohol, at this early age. It left a lasting impression on my young mind.

I know I felt very alone and insecure as a child, and maybe even a bit depressed. There was fun and crack at the meitheal, as well as the attention from the men, which I liked as a child. I always felt apart from this world, always feeling sad and lonely when the threshing was over and everyone had moved on to the neighbour's haggard to thresh their crops. I never wanted the party to be over.

By the age of fifteen, I had started to work part-time for local farmers. Finally, I had some money in my pocket. It was then that I started to go out to the local town, to the marquee at first. The marquee was a large, canvas tent erected every Easter and again in the summer, for the local festivals. There was a non-alcoholic bar, and some of the country's top showbands played there. My sisters and I were allowed to go some nights. I had not started drinking at this stage. Inside this big canvass tent, the girls stood on one side and the boys on the other. The boys had to walk over and ask the girls out to dance. It was a scary setup, and you could be rejected if the girl didn't like you. I got rejected many times. As a result, I felt shy and awkward, finding it increasingly difficult to put myself forward and ask any girl to dance. I was very self-conscious and didn't know how to dance. I didn't want people to laugh at me. I just didn't feel good enough about myself or confident at that time. The rejection was perceived as confirmation that I was not a nice person. I began to withdraw and my feet seemed heavier than ever.

One night, my old buddy Paddy, who is now passed away as a direct result of alcohol, had a bottle of whiskey in his pocket. He gave me a mouthful and at first I nearly got sick, as I didn't like the smell or taste of it. But within a few minutes—wow. I could feel it hitting my stomach with a burning sensation, then right up to my head. I felt a bit dizzy at first, but excited. It was like a bolt of lightning inside me, energising me. I lit up like a pinball machine. It was so electric, like being plugged into a personality changing machine. Immediately, I demanded more, and Paddy gave me some more. Within a short time, I felt ten feet tall and like I could jump over the moon, but most importantly at last I felt at ease, confident, more comfortable, and happier. It had transformed me.

I now walked confidently towards the line of girls waiting to be asked to dance. Self-doubt and fear never crossed my mind. I picked the finest looking girl and whisked her away up the floor. Michael Flatley would have been envious of my dancing. It was a total transformation. A few hours before, I was scared to ask a girl to dance and felt like I had concrete feet. Now, I was totally confident and the best dancer in the marquee (or so I thought). This was the effect alcohol had on me. It was amazing, like a miracle drug. I was never quite the same after that night out. That was when I discovered alcohol was something I could trust to make me feel better. It blew my toxic shame out of the water. Something had changed within me. The seed, planted eight or nine years previous, had finally sprouted.

I now believe I'd become addicted straight away. I remember it vividly, looking back; from that night on, alcohol was in the forefront of my mind. I became obsessed with it, daydreaming at school about getting out at the weekend, and losing interest in school and sports. I worked hard from a very young age so I'd have money for alcohol. I looked upon it as my saviour, but I was its slave, and it became my master within a few short years. My whole life centred around alcohol. Nothing else was as important as getting alcohol. It took me out of my self-consciousness. It freed me in a way nothing else could free me from my fears, my doubts, my inadequacies, and my inferiority complex. However, it was only a temporary fix, as the moment I put alcohol to my lips, something happened in my brain and my body craved for more. That craving is the most powerful thing I have ever experienced.

I lost all sense of control and reasoning, and the more I drank, the drunker I got, until I collapsed somewhere or ran out of money. I just could not understand how, when I took a drink of alcohol, I would lose all control of the amount I drank. My body could not tolerate much alcohol, and so I got drunk very quickly. I convinced my parents to let me drop out of school and get a fulltime job at seventeen, to which they reluctantly agreed. Now I had plenty of money for booze.

That's when my drinking escalated to a new level. I could afford to drink four nights a week now. Within six months, I was missing days off work and drinking in early morning pubs. I lost that job after eighteen months. This was to be the pattern for the next seventeen years. Going for a night out saying, "This time I won't get drunk, I'll only drink beer." Once I had one drink, I'd lose all control, getting drunk, having blackouts, and waking up aimlessly wandering in the early hours of the morning. Coming out of a blackout was very like when The Incredible Hulk came down off his rampage. My clothes would be dirty or torn or bloodstained. I wouldn't remember what had happened the night before. Back then, I knew I was in trouble with alcohol, but I was also in denial and always promised myself that if anything worse happened to me, I would stop drinking for good. But to be totally honest, I couldn't ever imagine life without alcohol.

I was a very strong willed person, who when I decided not to do something, it was practically written in stone. Little did I realise that no matter how much willpower I had, I had no power when it came to alcohol. My mind was incapable of recalling the last disastrous drinking episode, and so I was away on the next binge. I was, and still am, powerless over alcohol but didn't even realise it at that point. I found it impossible, after many attempts, to stop at different times, and so I spent the next seventeen years trying to control my drinking but failed miserably. There were brief moments where I thought I had regained control, but they were brief and usually followed by even worse binges, memory loss, and blackouts. I tried many ways to control my drinking, from having fish oil, milk, or dry bread before drinking alcohol. I tried not drinking spirits, pacing my drinks, drinking low alcohol beer, and any new ideas my drinking buddies would suggest. Sometimes, I might remember the earlier part of the night, but by the end of it I would be in a blackout. I would never remember anything about where I was or who I was talking to. After every binge, fear and guilt followed. I might bump into someone who saw me the night before, and they might say something like, "You were in some state last night," and laugh it off, but I wouldn't be laughing. Fear and shame would punch me so hard in the stomach that I'd feel sick and cringe.

Chapter 6

The Accident

It was a lovely, sunny July day here in the west of Ireland. I had started my own business selling confectionery and had been on the road all day selling. I was great at my job, I could sell anything with my charming ways, yet I felt this gnawing sickening feeling in my stomach. I was drinking most nights as I was making plenty of cash. However, I was not paying the supplier for the goods I was selling and this caused me to be fearful and anxious. I couldn't wait to run into the bar and get my anaesthetic. My dear dad had bailed me out of trouble once again, and had set me up with a van to start this new business as I was spoiled. In hindsight, it was like giving it to a 15 year old boy. I was twenty-four years old with a promising future ahead of me—if only I had matured like the average person and if only I could control the amount of alcohol I consumed. But, unfortunately neither was the case and the alcoholic seed had stalled my emotional growth, and now turned into a thriving plant that smothered everything I tried to accomplish.

Eighteen months previous, and I had been banned from driving for twelve months for drunk driving. I continued to drink and

drive drunk, walk sober

drive when I got my licence back. I was a danger to other road users but couldn't see it. I had failed to learn anything from that disqualification. The memory of that last ban was not enough to deter me from driving whilst drinking. Whenever I picked up a drink, all sense and reasoning departed. The stubborn streak in me ensured I had little respect for the law. I was selfish and self-centred. Looking back, I realise now I had a serious alcohol problem. I was seldom mildly drunk, but almost always seriously intoxicated.

My tolerance for alcohol was low. I was told many times by many people that I couldn't handle alcohol and that it didn't suit me. When drunk, I was convinced I was sober and often wondered what all the fuss was about. People had taken car keys off me after a row on several occasions. I could not get it into my head that I was incapable of driving when I drank alcohol. It made no sense in my head. My mind was incapable of registering my drunken state, as I was convinced I was sober. It was crazy. I was immature and couldn't picture life without it. When sober, I was still shy and a bit uncomfortable around people. The alcohol initially gave me the confidence I lacked and a sense of ease. I was restless, moody, and generally unhappy.

I vaguely remember going into the bar on the evening of the accident. I had become friends with a local girl called Mary. She was having a going away party, as she was emigrating to America the following day. It made me sad that she had to emigrate. I think it was around five o'clock when I went to the bar. The only other thing I remember after that, is Mary playing pool. I cannot recall anything else that happened that evening. I was aware I had a going away present for her at home. It was a soft toy, and it was in my head to go home, get the present, and come back again. But I don't remember leaving the bar or anything else. As usual, I was in a blackout. I obviously drove the van but never arrived home, instead waking up in hospital the following morning and remembering nothing. Years later, Mary informed me I just disappeared from the pub and nobody knew where I had gone until they heard the tragic news shortly after.

Looking back I never had the luxury of social drinking, because I drank alcoholically from day one. Any small bit of pleasure I received from the first few drinks was soon cancelled out by me getting out of control and into a blackout. Most normal drinkers stop when they feel themselves getting too drunk, but not the alcoholic. They just want more and more. According to some research, the alcoholic does not break down alcohol as efficiently as a normal drinker. A chemical called tetrahydroisoquinoline is produced in the brain of the alcoholic, which is more addictive than morphine and which I will discuss in more detail later.

I spent all my life looking to alcohol for the feeling of friendship, fun, and belonging I'd had as a boy at the threshing mill. But that feeling was long gone. Depression had taken its place now. It was like hitting myself on the head with a hammer, hoping it would cure a headache. The more I got drunk, the more guilt and shame I buried within myself when I sobered up the next day. I didn't want to be this way. I just wanted to go out and socialise like everyone else and drink like a normal person, but that was impossible. I could never have one or two drinks and walk away.

It was only after years in recovery that I realised how insane my mind was when alcohol was involved. By now, I had become totally dependent on alcohol. It was like a double-edged sword. It gave me temporary relief from myself and the reality I had created from blindly bulldozing my way through life on one hand, and on the other it terrorised me with fear, shame, and guilt when I was dry. I couldn't imagine life without it, but in the last few years of my drinking, I couldn't picture life with or without alcohol. It was like a merry-go-round. Something bad seemed to happen every time I drank. At times, it was small and the shame wasn't too bad, but there was always guilt and shame after every session. That was my life for seventeen years. I was just going around and around in a circle, getting paid, going out, and getting drunk in spite of desperately not wanting to. I'd sober up, get more depressed and ashamed, bury that deep down within myself, lose jobs, get back to work, and repeat the whole scenario. This went on and on for all those years, in the prime of my life.

I also had many sweet relationships, only to be lost as a direct result of alcohol. As time went on, the relationships got fewer and fewer, until there was nobody in my life and I was totally alone. Alcohol was the great remover. By the time I stopped, I was overloaded with negative feelings. However, some powerful yet faint voice in my head constantly reminded me I had to get away from this or go crazy.

It took seventeen years of alcoholic drinking to finally throw in the towel and concede, I could no longer drink in safety. I wish I could say I stopped drinking before the unthinkable happened, but the unthinkable did happen, and the effects of my alcoholism would nearly drive me crazy.

Chapter 7

Turning Point

The last accident I had, when I crashed into a herd of cows, was the end of the road for me. I was still half drunk from the night before. Some of the animals were injured and lay there on the road. The loud bang of the impact reminded me of the accident with Paul. The noise of it brought everything back to me. There was a horrible feeling in the pit of my stomach. I knew in my heart and soul that I couldn't carry on living like that anymore.

A moment of clarity emerged. My whole existence played out in slow motion right before my eyes. It was crystal clear. It was as if I was standing outside of myself, looking at this wreck of a man with his life in tatters. Suddenly, I instinctively knew the game was up. I realised I had to stop hiding and admit that I was beaten, I needed help, and I could not recover on my own. This was the beginning of the end for that life; what I can only describe as a spiritual awakening.

This was the turning point, the beginning of recovery for me. After the accident with the cows, I knew I had to reach out and get help. In all those years of alcoholism, I had gone from

drive drunk, walk sober

a good, loving, caring, respectful young teenager, to a self-centred, withdrawn, depressed man. At the age of thirty-four, I had the mindset and social skills of a fifteen-year-old boy, incapable of relating properly to anyone. Having not grown and matured, I was totally dysfunctional, opting to play with the dog or kids, rather than hold an adult conversation. My emotional growth was stunted. All I could think of was alcohol and how to get enough of it to get relief from this reality.

I had reached yet another rock bottom. After the accident with the cows, something awoke within me, and I somehow knew deep down within myself this was the end of my drinking. I arrived back at my room in the doss house and broke down. My head was going crazy. I wanted to smash it against the wall, the mental pain was so bad. I felt guilty, afraid, frustrated, hopeless, and angry. I thought of suicide, as the emotional turmoil was unbearable, but I had tried that before and failed twice. I could not tolerate the emotional pain, so I decided to go to the bar. After all, it was the only solution I knew. On my way to the bar, I had a feeling this was not the answer, but it was the only way I knew of anesthetizing the mental torture. I prayed to whatever power was out there to help me. I had one drink and then many more, but there was a knowing in me that alcohol was no longer the solution. Alcohol no longer anaesthetised me like it used to. I walked out of that bar still sober but depressed, then went back to my little man cave. As I lied on the bed, I looked around the small room. It was a dirty magnolia in colour. There were no pictures on the walls, no designer clothes in the wardrobe, and I had nothing to show for my seventeen years of hard work but misery. I couldn't bear the reality of it all. I was compelled by the physical craving for alcohol to go back to the bar. The plan in my head was to drink whatever money I had left, and then jump into the local river that night and end it all. My thinking was that I would no longer be a burden to anyone.

Whatever powers that were out there obviously had different plans for me, because when all my money was gone, and I had sucked out every ounce of anaesthetic from the alcohol, my sister appeared out of nowhere. She ordered me into her car and took me to her home.

I was at my lowest point ever, I was scared I'd lose my mind and commit suicide in the middle of the night. I couldn't sleep and was having withdrawal symptoms. My then girlfriend spent the night with me in my sister's house. I managed to get through the night and the next day, I called the local addiction treatment centre. An appointment was made for two days later, but I thought on that morning, *"No, no, I don't need this, sure I'm not too bad, I'll get over this."* Deep down, I knew if I didn't go then, God only knew what would happen next. I went to the appointment and told my story, they diagnosed me as a chronic alcoholic. I was shocked, yet relieved, to hear it from professionals. Hearing it from my family and girlfriends was upsetting but didn't have the same impact on me. Most people had said I should cop myself on and pull myself together, but now I was finally diagnosed with the disease of alcoholism.

Then, the disease whispered in my ear *"Maybe they're lying, maybe they just want to make money out of you."* Paranoid thoughts were part of the insanity going on in my head after all that had happened over the past seventeen years of drinking. After the interview, they told me there was a month waiting list, and that I'd have to stay dry for the next month. I thought I'd never last but just took it day by day. They told me to call every week just in case someone had not shown up. I called after the first week and they told me to come in straight away, as there was a bed available. I was overjoyed, because I was finding it increasingly difficult to fight off the alcoholic thoughts. I ran in the door that day like a scared rat. I desperately needed to get off the street. Now, I was a resident in an addiction treatment centre for thirty days.

The treatment centre was like a five-star hotel. The food was first class, and the whole place was luxurious. I was very emotional the first day I arrived, and felt I didn't deserve this kind of luxury after all the damage I had done. With my constant companions, guilt, self-pity, and toxic shame, I found it hard to accept anyone's kindness. I didn't trust anyone at this stage and was very sceptical of the whole setup. The staff councillors, especially the two ladies who founded the place, Elaine and Patricia, were kind and respectful towards me. I found that difficult to accept. When you drink alcoholically for many years, respect is not something you expect to receive from others. Somehow, I knew I was in the right place and for the first time since prison, I felt safe and secure.

There was a lot of work to be done. I knew that if I didn't do something then, I'd be finished. This was a great opportunity for me to straighten my life out. I was desperate to recover, and there was something intrinsic within me that reinforced a belief that there was a better life out there. That driving force, or power, kept me going even in the lowest times. That power picked me up and drove me forward, no matter what came up. The first week in the treatment centre was okay; nothing much happened for me. I was unconsciously putting up resistance to their concepts and recovery. I wanted to cling to the old survival methods I was familiar with. I had a lot of self-pity after being in victim mode for the past ten years.

Turning Point

While in group therapy, we talked about a lot of heavy emotional stuff, and I felt like an outsider looking in at the seven other people in treatment. I was in denial a lot of the time. I was incapable of connecting with the accident. It was like I was frozen. I knew I had that accident and Paul was killed with two others injured, but it was like it had happened to someone else. I had buried it so deep within myself that it wouldn't see the light of day ever again. However, I wanted desperately to feel the pain of it. I wanted to try and deal with it somehow, so I could accept what had happened, pick up the pieces, and move forward with what was left of this life of mine.

I had drowned the accident out with alcohol for many years and it would take a miracle for it to surface. I felt numb inside. I was scared to let it up, but I knew if I didn't, I would never recover, and this thirty days of treatment would be a waste of time.

Then, something powerful happened. We were shown a short video of a drunk driver causing a fatal accident that evening. Suddenly, I got this sick feeling in my stomach. I had to run outside and vomit, with years of smothered emotions coming up and out. I was vomiting and crying for what seemed like ages. It felt like I was drinking again; my body was shaking, it was like a volcano had erupted inside me. The realisation of having the accident played out in my mind. This was the first time since the morning in the hospital bed I had really connected with what had happened. The feelings had been buried alive for over 10 years. Someone held me in their arms as I cried like a baby, while what seemed like buckets of tears flowed out. There was no noise now, just water flowing from my eyes. I believe my body let go of the trauma that evening.

Then there was silence, and I was in the present moment. My mind was crystal clear and silent. I believe I had another spiritual experience that evening. I went to bed and slept twelve hours without waking up, I was so exhausted. On awaking, reality punched me in the stomach. The beautiful peace I had the night before had disappeared, and I knew I had work to do. The one thing that was different, was that now I had hope. It was a great beginning. I was now determined to do the best I could. I was told to relax, let go of my own old ideas, and just listen.

There was no resistance left in me. I became vulnerable for the first time since going to Paul's mother to make amends. Vulnerability is the greatest measure of courage. It is emotional risk, exposure, the birthplace of change. The following three weeks, I worked closely with my councillor on the damage I had caused. I had a victim attitude. To recover that attitude needed to change to gratitude. Gratitude was something I never practised or was hardly aware of. It is the antidote to self-pity.

Many questions arose that were hard to answer. Could I have avoided the other car? Why did I not see it coming? Was I really on the wrong side of the road? Why wasn't I seriously injured? Why did I escape with only flesh wounds? Did I survive physically, but not mentally? The accident took its toll on me too, and I might as well have died that night. Why didn't I die? Has God got a sick sense of humour? Is there really a God in it all? Why can I not let this go and forgive myself? What can I do now to change one single thing about the past? Is it possible to wake up some morning and not think of what happened? I left nothing out.

The feelings of not deserving any peace or happiness were very strong. I had a judge who whipped me any time I felt joy or love. It had kept me down for all those years, that punishing judge who never even took a day off. I learned it was shame and that there were two types of shame, normal shame and toxic shame. It was a revelation to me to discover this toxic shame. I could accept I was unintentionally wounded as a child by almost everyone I came in contact with, especially teachers and the church. Toxic shame made me feel like I wasn't worthy or good enough as a person. It explained why I felt not good enough all my life from as far back as I can remember. Toxic shame can only be healed by coming out of hiding, talking about what's going on in your head and trying to replace negative beliefs with positive ones. Empathy is the only antidote to toxic shame.

It was toxic shame, ever watchful and vigilant, always whispering in my ear, *You don't deserve anything, you scumbag. You killed Paul, remember? You cannot be happy or joyful after what you did. You are not equal to everyone else. Don't even think you are deserving, because you are not. You are just a piece of shit.*

It was a savage merciless voice that had controlled me all of my life and was reinforced by every trauma I had ever experienced.

I discovered that this voice—this monster—was common for addicts. They even had a special name for it in the treatment centre. It was called "Slick." I realised Slick was a spokesman for the toxic shame I lived with all my life.

How could I be aware of and deal with this monster? Slick was permanently perched on my shoulder, whispering into my ear. He had become my master and seemed like a real part of me. I wanted to be able to leave this place with hopes for a new start. This accident had now defined me. I would introduce myself as Sean and secretly say to myself, *The one who had the accident*. It was always in the back of my mind, but awareness and self-examination was the first step for me. Whenever I felt bad, I had to become aware it was Slick representing the toxic shame, at work whispering in my ear. It was only when I'd get glimpses of hope and happiness, that I would become aware that Slick was silent; something else was working in my life. Gradually, I chose to not entertain him and not feed him with negative emotion. I discovered this was what he lived on, and I had been overfeeding him all those years, until he had become very large, indeed.

I also became aware that I loved feeling sorry for myself. I got a morbid sense of pleasure out of it. It was learned in childhood. It was "poor this" and "poor that" in our home. I had wallowed in the memory of this accident for over ten years at this point, but it was time to stop. It wasn't helping anyone, but only killing me. I was told I needed to practise gratitude, but I couldn't think of anything to be grateful for; it was a great excuse for me to feel sorry for myself.

Gradually, I discovered that something greater than Slick was also present within me. It was a silent, all powerful presence. At first, there were only tiny glimpses this power. It was like a small light, smothered with negative emotions. If this light was to shine, then these negative emotions would have to be examined and removed. I worked hard on these while I was there, but a lifetime of negativity couldn't be sorted in three weeks. Luckily, I had two years of aftercare and a twelve-step programme to turn to after I left the treatment centre. Then,

Turning Point

the day came when it was time to leave the security of the treatment centre and get back to the real world. The only thing I was one-hundred-percent sure of on leaving the treatment centre, was that I could no longer drink in safety. My drinking days would be over, one day at a time. I also felt hope and had my new tools for coping and living in reality without my anaesthetic.

As I arrived in my home town after thirty days in treatment, fear gripped me again. Slick was back in force, this time screaming in my ear, *You can't handle this, do you think you are cured now, ya scumbag? You will NEVER change. You might as well go for drink. You have a few pounds dole coming to ya. Go to the pub, there you will find relief.* I was in shock, and I was confused. For the first time in the real world, I became aware of slick at work. These were the horrible messages I was listening to all my life, even before I ever picked up alcohol, and it was all toxic shame. By now, I could take a step back and realise what was happening. This was a revelation for me, as I realised I had lived all my life unconsciously under the dictates of Slick. But now I was also more conscious of that silent presence within me. I was armed with this newly found power, yet very shaky on my legs, like a new born lamb. The most important thing I learned in the treatment centre, was that there was no solution in alcohol. It was all over. I was convinced of this after intensive treatment. All this work I had done on myself would have been futile had I had surrendered to Slick's demands. My mind was crystal clear on this. Sanity prevailed, and I called to a friend instead and told him what was going on with me. He sat me down, and we talked until Slick faded away into the distance for that day.

drive drunk, walk sober

It was the first time I ever stood up and challenged this voice in my head. I was delighted, with the help of some likeminded friends and my new-found power and knowledge, that I got through that day without a drink. Up until I write here now, I have never had a craving for alcohol since. It has been removed from me, like I never drank it in the first place. It's a miracle and due to trusting that power within me, sticking with a group of like-minded friends, and practising using the set of tools for living in all my dealings with others. I strictly take it one day at a time, and I'm constantly aware Slick is still there waiting for the right opportunity to get me back drinking. All I have is a daily reprieve from alcohol. I am not cured, as there is no known cure for alcoholism.

I was back out there in the real world. I was raw, scared, and vulnerable. A lot had happened in the last thirty days. I was a new man after offloaded the guilt and remorse. I was still very fragile though and doubted myself. I had been given a new set of tools for living sober, but like any new tools, I had to practise using them. Although the alcohol problem had been removed, there was a long period of reconstruction ahead; lots of pain and emotional turmoil. My life was a shambles, I was a wreck and "Rome wasn't built in a day," they say. The first thing I had to learn was to take my time and be patient, kind, and compassionate with myself and allow for setbacks, accepting my imperfections.

The greatest occupier of my mind was the accident. Because of my impatient nature, I wanted to try and heal the pain of it straight away. Looking back now, because of past conditioning, this would take time. Learning to accept that there was nothing I could do to change one single thing about the accident was hard. It meant just letting go and trusting this new-found power. I did not want to let go of punishing myself. Because I was steeped in toxic shame, I couldn't let go and let that silent power take care of things. It was going to take time. Because of my strong will and determination, I tried to force things. The more I pushed, the more painful it got. I realise now this was a healing process that took time, no matter how I tried to bulldoze my way through. Part of the recovery programme was to make amends wherever possible, except when it would cause further harm. How could I make amends to Paul after causing his death? I wanted to make amends sooner rather than later as the pain and guilt of what had happened was savage, now that I had no anaesthetic, and I was not great at tolerating pain. The fact that I could no longer escape the pain frustrated me.

The impatience within me was driving me on, and I learned from the treatment centre that impatience was a character defect of mine, so I needed to slow down, get silent, and listen. Then, one of my friends suggested I write him a letter, read it at his grave, and then burn it. I thought that was a great idea and set about writing a letter to Paul, explaining the disease and how sorry I was to be the cause of taking his life. I had to write this on my own, and it was very difficult. The old guilt, toxic shame, and remorse were being reinforced by Slick, but I managed to write it. I had never been to Paul's grave; I just couldn't face going when I was still drinking. It was too painful to face, and by not going, it didn't seem as real.

Now I was sober maybe five months, I felt a little stronger and decided to go. I remember it was a cool September day. It was now over ten years since the accident. I arrived at the graveyard but didn't even know where Paul's grave was. I'd never had the strength and courage to visit Paul's grave before this. I didn't tell anyone I was going; I didn't want anyone to know. This was a journey I had to make alone. I had to face Paul alone. I walked up and down the rows of headstones and went back through the years on them. I was looking for 1985, but a lot of people had passed away since Paul. Then, suddenly, I stumbled upon his little grave. I felt the usual sickening feeling in my stomach. My heart was broken—I was broken. It was so upsetting and real. I wished I had my anaesthetic. I thought of Paul's little body there, underneath the ground. It was the closest I had come to him physically since the accident. I didn't really know what to expect. I saw his name engraved into the headstone. Now, his death was very real. This was the legacy of my alcoholism. I was overcome with grief.

A hurricane of emotions of guilt and sadness ran riot in my head, and tears flowed freely. I felt very ashamed. There was a lot of regret and sadness. I just kneeled and stared at the grave for ages. I read out my apology. *Sure, what good's a letter now?* Slick whispered in my ear. There were some flowers growing on there. I wished I had brought flowers. Slick whispered, *Sure, what good are flowers now you asshole? Why don't you just dig down and crawl into the grave with him?* And then I realised this Slick had me hammered again. I finished my apology, despite those interjections, and then asked for Paul's forgiveness. I then said a prayer. It was like I had met Paul for the first time. It was sad yet peaceful.

I was emotional after leaving the graveyard. I drove around aimlessly for what seemed like hours, immersed in raw grief, anger, guilt, and regret. I was trying to let go of more guilt and painful emotions attached to the accident. Not once did it occur to me to pick up a drink. No, I never even thought about that. A spiritual awakening had happened in the treatment centre, and it was holding out good. Some more healing around the accident had taken place. I thought it was all over, that I had dealt with this now, and that would be the end of it. However, coming out of the treatment centre and staying sober was only the beginning. Recovery from alcoholism is a lifetime journey.

Chapter 8

The Toxic Shame Game

There are two types of shame: *healthy shame* and *toxic shame*.

Healthy shame starts in childhood and helps you create boundaries. Healthy shame is about being okay with making mistakes, being real, being human, and asking for help. Healthy shame is realising I have limits and can't do everything on my own. Healthy shame gives me permission to be human. Healthy shame is the source of humility and spirituality. When I accept that I am powerless, then I realise a power greater than me is present in my life. We all need a sense of shame, and it helps us function normally in this world. If I don't have healthy shame, I'm not in touch with my basic boundary. Healthy shame is permission to be human. Healthy shame lets me know I need other people; that I need love and support. Healthy shame is also the source of creativity and learning. It is the highest form of self respect to admit mistakes and make amends for them. That's healthy shame in action.

Toxic shame, however, is more a state of being. I cannot remember a time in my childhood when I didn't feel ashamed

drive drunk, walk sober

of myself in some form or another. It was the single root cause of my alcoholism. Empathy is the antidote to toxic shame. I learned about shame in the family home and when I started going to school, and then the church also conditioned me into believing I was flawed and unworthy. Toxic shame is silent and secretive. Shame-based people go into hiding. Shame-based people, because of feeling unworthy, believe they don't deserve to depend on anyone for help and support. Toxic shame is feeling disgraced about who I am. Shame-based people cannot be of much support to others until they come out of hiding. Toxic shame is spiritual bankruptcy. I had to try and control the outcome of everything in my life. I could not depend on someone else or on my power within. Toxic shame violates healthy shame. Healthy shame admits your limited—toxic shame says you must be perfect. Toxic shame expects perfection from an imperfect person. Toxic shame stifles creativity. Toxic shame hates exposure.

According to John Bradshaw, "Every addiction is rooted in toxic shame. Every addict has the core belief that they are flawed and defective as human beings."[1] This was my core limiting belief.

First, I had to investigate where the toxic shame originated without blaming anyone. I went back to a time when I was very young. I vaguely remember being in the cot in front of a mirror. It was a light blue cot and I used to chew the rail on top. I liked looking at the teeth marks I left in the rail. I can still taste the paint to this day. From talking to my mother about this I discovered she would place me in the cot in front of the wardrobe mirror, then sneak out of the room and go to the fields to help my father. She told me I'd cry for a while

---

[1] Bradsaw, John. *Healing the Shame that Binds You*. HCI, 2005.

and then go to sleep. I remember feeling alone even at that age and trying to escape my prison. I believe the toxic shame may have begun there. I think I must have perceived this as abandonment. I must have developed a feeling of not being worth my mother's time or love. When she'd disappear, I think I lost trust in her. I do not blame her, as we are all victims of victims. Also, we lived on a farm and there was always plenty of work to be done, with no time for nurturing anyone. Children were a bi-product of unprotected sex and were just another set of hands to work on the farm.

Throughout my life, I had that feeling of unworthiness, isolation, loneliness, and depression. When children get no time or nurturing from parents, they look upon themselves as being worth less than their parents time and, because this becomes so painful, they develop a false self. All my life, it was like there were two of us: me and this harsh, judgemental self, watching my every move and judging me.

Now, I know him to be Slick, toxic shame's spokesman. We are born perfect, but whenever something traumatic happens, we lose that spontaneity and that love. In a toxic shame based family, all rules are strict and rigid. We were not supposed to make mistakes in our family. If we did make mistakes, we were duly punished and informed it was our own fault. In other words, I learned from an early age that I couldn't expect love or support in my family, and so I became a prime candidate for addictions that gave me relief from this toxic shame. The big one for me was feeling unworthy. I could say to myself *I am worthy of being loved and cared for*, but secretly I'd cringe and not believe it. Even the church told me through the mass that I wasn't not worthy to receive the communion unless I repent. That was ingrained in my subconscious mind. All the destruction I caused in my active addiction also reaffirmed how bad a person I was, and how I deserved nothing but punishment.

There were eight of us in the family: four boys and four girls. It was a busy farming household. There was always lots of work to be done. There was no time for sitting down and talking about your feelings. It was frowned upon and looked upon as being soft and weak. I was a worrier and took everything way too seriously. I took "everything to heart," and I was always reminded of this growing up. We were a family full of fear and worry, afraid of failure, afraid of not having enough money, and afraid of what the neighbours might think. There was no time for nurturing children. That was a no-no. We got some nurturing from my father, mainly if we were sick. Years later when the accident happened, I couldn't talk about it, especially to my family. Toxic shame ensured there would be little compassion or support as far as everyone was concerned.

People who suffer from toxic shame act shamelessly, have no boundaries, and cannot say no. They are rigid perfectionists, blaming themselves for everything, with no room for mistakes. When I embraced the toxic shame within me, I recovered. I had to journey inward to that inner child and become a parent to myself. Today, I love and respect myself and nurture the little Sean inside. It is only with a sense of trust that a child can develop a sense of *healthy* shame. They cannot be shamed by someone they don't care about. There must be a sense of relating on the child's part to have healthy shame. And so, if the child has this feeling of love and trust, they develop the ability to say no and set boundaries. I didn't have that sense of trust as a child growing up.

The Toxic Shame Game

Creating trust in a power greater than Slick was a major step in recovery for me. Once I started to nurture, love, and take care of the child within me, I began to feel good and say no when I needed to. This was the beginning of recovery for me, but I first had to surrender, to give up trying to control everything, to come out of hiding, join like-minded people in recovery, start sharing how I felt, get lots of counselling, learn to love myself, ask for what I wanted, and make a beginning on trusting something greater than my ego; share my fears, resentments and guilt with this power and another person, make amends for harms done and learn to live this new way of life. The more I practise it, the more positive thinking becomes part of my life.

I realise now, all my addictions were an outer reach for inner security.

It was then the journey of discovery started for me. First, I learned I have a belief system. It's like a book of rules programmed into me from birth. This belief system determined how I lived my life and the crazy thing was they weren't even my beliefs, but the beliefs of my parents, peers, teachers, and basically anyone I had contact with since birth. Some were early childhood beliefs that I naturally outgrew, like Santa clause, and another one was putting salt on a rabbit's tail so I could catch one. My father lovingly instilled that one in me, and I also believed I came from under a head of cabbage, until I eventually figured out where I really came from and how it all started through observing the animals on the farm. The church instilled the belief that even thinking of sex was a sin, so I believed l was a sinner from the age of twelve, therefore reinforcing my toxic shame.

The beliefs I held were subtle yet powerful. It was almost impossible to become aware of them while I was in active addiction, because I was totally immersed in them and didn't know any different. They were my default settings from a young age. How was I to heal from this toxic shame?

First, I had to be reprogrammed. The treatment centre made a beginning. It's easier to see the mountain clearly when you're standing some distance away from it. Through meditation, I learned to step back from my mind and become aware of my thinking. This helped me to stop and look at what thoughts I was focusing on. I was slowly waking up; becoming aware. I remember reading a book called *As a Man Thinketh* by James Allen. Wow, it was a revelation to me, realising whatever thoughts I focused on created a feeling inside me and that feeling determined how I behaved. How I then behaved created more feelings and that created similar thoughts to the original ones, and so it was a crazy merry-go-round. It was so simple, I had missed it all my life. I presumed I knew it all until then, but I was only fulfilling my limited beliefs unconsciously, which originated in the toxic shame, and therefore hoping I'd get pity from someone. It was a vicious cycle. The accident was proof for me, confirming my limiting beliefs about being a worthless human being, and enabled me to carry on punishing and pitying myself, and prolonging the guilt for over ten years. I was not at ease, but alcohol was the only anaesthetic I knew of that gave me temporary respite from this disease.

Identifying limiting beliefs in myself was no easy task at first, until I learned my actions were the manifestations of what I really believed. It wasn't until I got into treatment that I realised I was running my life on other people's beliefs; they belonged to my parents and peers, unknowingly passed on to me as a child. It was then, I began to question why I felt so unworthy and unlovable. Every time I became aware I was telling myself I was a bad person, I had to stop and challenge the thought. It was difficult, as my mind was on autopilot and the accident confirmed to me that I was an unworthy person. My ego, or Slick, would then proceed to strengthen that limiting belief within me. I believed I was no good, would never be any good, and that nobody liked me after what I'd done. It was difficult to challenge, with so much concrete evidence confirming these beliefs.

The basic law of perception states that "You see what you believe is there and you believe it's there because you want it there." I saw I was a worthless person because of all the failures I created, and I then believed I was worthless by confirming all these failures, because toxic shame had me convinced I was worthless. I wanted to believe this about me because it was all I knew all my life.

By carefully looking at my actions today, I can see what I really believe about myself. My thoughts, feelings, and actions reflect how I behave in this world today. So, it's important for me to be silent and observe what's going on in this head of mine.

It took a lot of time and energy before my beliefs about myself changed. I was in recovery from alcoholism for at least two years, before I realised this belief system was a cycle, first entertaining a negative thought, believing it to be true without questioning it, and then acting it out. I had unconsciously lived this way all my life. Awareness was the key. I became aware of the thoughts I was focusing on and came to realise those negative beliefs could be replaced with positive ones, but also that I was more than just my beliefs. It took a lot of self-examination, repetition, affirmations, and acting as if they were true before I had any success. I get to create my own reality today by creating an image of what I want to become, focusing on positive beliefs, and trusting my power with the best possible outcome. As soon as I become aware a belief is not serving me I then replace it with something more positive. I was over two and a half years in recovery, before I began to see the results of my hard work. The first tangible evidence of this working in my life was being able to stop smoking: my first major addiction. I began to like and care about myself and didn't like it when I inhaled smoke into my lungs. That new belief gave me the willingness and motivation to quit smoking for good. It was a long road back, and this was the first milestone for me. Then, I became aware of other beliefs that didn't serve me as I began to like myself.

When I was four years into recovery, I decided to start up my own business. The limiting belief that I was no good, and that I'd fail in business, came to the surface. I had to challenge that, and I remember saying to slick, *You can say what you want, but I'm going to do this anyway, and I will not fail.* I noticed that when I went ahead with my plans, Slick became less powerful. A year later, I got a mortgage and built my own home.

I also examined my core values and came to recognise where the beliefs I held were clashing with these. Core values are the guiding principles that dictate our behaviour and actions. A value is a measure of the worth or importance a person attaches to something. Values are intangible, yet visible to others. We are born with principles that guide us and determine how we relate in this world. I value respect, honesty, loyalty, love, nature, etc. Because of toxic shame and negative belief systems, my values were not honoured. This caused me to feel depressed, angry, and sad.

Today, my values and belief systems work in harmony with each other, and I have great moments of peace. I feel at ease with people and the world most of the time. I practise gratitude now instead of self-pity. I trust my higher self instead of being fearful. While I make plans, I also try to live in the moment as much as I can and not try and control the outcome. I have made many mistakes since I stopped drinking, but I prefer to look on them as lessons learned and try not to repeat them however I have healthy shame today and realise I'm not perfect, just another human being . I have had more emotional growing pains in the last twenty years than I ever had while drinking. I have recovered from a hopeless state of mind but only have a daily reprieve from alcohol. I know if I pick up alcohol today, it will kill me. I am under no illusion, because I cannot handle it, so I respect that. Alcohol is not an issue today. I am restored to sanity regarding alcohol today. I am free and very grateful.

Staying sober, one day at a time, and being aware of Slick is my number one priority now. Sometimes, he catches me off guard but not for long. After twelve years of learning to live in the real world, my dear dad passed away. He is buried in the same graveyard as Paul. The day we took my father to his final resting place, I had to pass by Paul's grave once more. It was the first time I was there in twelve years. After my father's burial was over and everyone had left, I revisited Paul's grave. This time, there was pain but not as severe as the first time. The wound had healed a bit but the scar remains. I had come to realise over the twelve years in recovery that yes, I was responsible for Paul's death. I was driving the van that night.

drive drunk, walk sober

My senses were impaired because of alcohol. Slick had caught me off guard. Some of the old shame and guilt came pouring back into my mind. I don't know how long I stayed at Paul's grave that day. I realised I will never forget what happened and that is the one thing I will live with for the rest of my days. Eventually, I left the graveyard feeling a bit sad for Paul's death and also sad for my dad's passing. Now I could turn to my power and trust that all would be ok. If I did not have the disease of alcoholism, that accident probably wouldn't have happened. Slick on my shoulder does not want me to ease up on myself. He wants me to punish myself for the rest of my days. Slick is toxic shame at its finest.

However, that small light within me is brighter now, and I have learned to accept the accident happened. Now, I understand that I am powerless to change the past. I have a healthy shame about it these days. I accept I caused it. The only amends I can make is to stay sober, one day at a time, and help others. I have learned I need to be compassionate with myself now, instead of being harsh and judgemental. I will always be deeply sorry for what happened to Paul, his brother Pat and Michael the driver. . Today, I am more aware that Slick can come back with a vengeance, especially If I lose trust in my inner power.

I came to realise life was hopeless and futile the way I was living it. I also became aware of self-pity. Having pity for self is a highly addictive non-pharmaceutical drug. I believed I was a victim all my life and expected condolences from everyone. I needed to stop nursing this self-pity. The first step was becoming aware of the belief I was a victim—I was feeling sorry for myself. I had learned that as a child. Pity will get you attention from your parents. I confused pity with love. I was looking outward for love through self-pity and getting resentful when my victim mentality was frowned upon, nowadays I find love within myself and everywhere around me, especially in nature. Gratitude is the only antidote to self-pity. Today, through being present and aware, I am responsible for the thoughts I choose to entertain in my wonderful mind. All those years of misery, I was looking for someone to rescue me, to lift me out of my miserable self. But nobody came to rescue this small child within me. So, I needed to grow up and parent myself. Today, I have a choice, but I need to make that choice every moment. I realise now that self-pity is highly addictive, and it gave me a morbid sense of pleasure, but separated me from reality. It took years in recovery to become aware I was in victim mode and to get gratitude into my life.

I was incapable of accepting the consequences of my drunken actions while I was still in active addiction. I wasted many years suffering because of alcoholism. I no longer feel a victim in this story.

Having examined my core values and limiting beliefs I feel better equipped to cope with the memory of causing Paul's death and also the trials of living in the real world today. I am grateful to have a second chance at life today and realise it's impossible to be full of self-pity and full of joy at the same time. However, it can be difficult to enjoy life when living with the memory of causing someone's death. There were brief moments where I would experience happiness and joy, and then the automatic negative beliefs kicked in. Slick would viciously whisper, *Hey, why are you being so happy, ya scumbag? Why are you happy after what you've done? You CANNOT be happy or joyful, you don't deserve to be happy ever again after what you've done, you will be judged by everyone else, as well. Now, get back to being shameful and miserable as that's all you deserve.* This internal dialogue was very familiar. I felt undeserving of any happiness or joy. Slick restrained me for many years in recovery. I was not free. I believed I had to suffer for the rest of my life and associated self-pity, pain, and guilt with repayment for wrong doings especially the accident. Whenever I did something wrong as a child, the words "shame on you" were quoted. Much later, I finally realised this belief just HAD TO GO. After the accident, I made the decision that shame, guilt, and low self-worth was the price I would pay for the rest of my days. This was the only ambition I had for myself. The thing is, I didn't become aware of this until I was at least two years into recovery. I had to define myself in a different, more positive way. I had to change the way I viewed the past. But how was I to learn to be happy and free even though I was sober? There was an invisible lead on me that yanked me back any time I began to feel joy or happiness. I still felt very guilty about the accident. The guilt I had after the accident served me in the short-term, but it was no longer serving me. Guilt is completely different to toxic shame. Guilt develops a lot later than shame. Guilt says you made a mistake, but toxic shame says you *are* a mistake. Guilt is about doing, but toxic shame is about being. Guilt can be healed by changing your actions. I used to confuse guilt with toxic shame. I thought they were similar. It was important for me to learn the difference between guilt and toxic shame. After the accident, I felt guilty but didn't realise it was the toxic shame prolonging the guilt. Until I became aware of this toxic shame, I could not forgive myself and let the accident go. I had to take responsibility for my own wounding; I had to admit I was suffering from toxic shame. I had learned all about guilt from a young age. There was a lot of manipulation and guilt imposed on me as a child. When I refused to do something I didn't want to do, I was manipulated into feeling guilty, which further reinforced the toxic shame and became a breeding ground for resentment. I even felt guilty for feeling happy or joyful and, therefore, could not allow myself to be in a joyful relationship or to just be happy. Because of toxic shame I felt unworthy of joy or happiness from a very young age. Alot of my guilt was connected to other people's emotions and expectations of me. How could I have known how other people felt or what they expected from me? I'd made a lot of assumptions, and it was really none of my business trying to guess. Guilt is about transgressing something I value and causing Paul's death was a huge violation of every value I held. Because I was such a good, kind, loving person behind all this toxic shame, and the fact that I had caused Paul's death made the guilt almost unbearable at times.

Guilt is not a bad emotion in itself, as it guides me to think and behave in a way that fits my own value system. It plays a productive role in my life these days. I stay sober one day at a time and try and help others because of positive guilt.

Appropriate guilt is a normal reaction when you do something wrong, however because of the toxic shame and my expectations of me having to be perfect, I ruminated over the guilt of causing the accident for over ten years and this caused self-directed resentment and caused me to sink deeper into depression. When you suffer from toxic shame mistakes are not allowed. But smothering the guilt with alcohol was never the answer. As soon as I'd sober up, the guilt, tinged with toxic shame, was back with a vengeance.

I believe I have forgiven myself, today. Slick still tries to tell me I'm a worthless human being, "Nobody will believe ya," he says. That old recording still arises from time to time but because I'm very much aware of it nowadays, it has no power over me. At first, I was shaky and doubted my power, but the longer I stay sober, the more I trust my all loving power within my heart and soul. The more I try to live a spiritual life by practising prayer and meditation the stronger my defence is against going back to a life of guilt and shame. My main purpose in life now is to be of service to others, to help others to recover from alcoholism and causing a fatal accident through addiction.

When I embraced the toxic shame within me, I recovered. I have journeyed inward to that little Sean and developed a relationship with him. Today I love, respect, and nurture myself. I take good care of that small boy within me. I have boundaries now and allow myself to make mistakes. It's been an amazing journey and continues to grow and develop.

Vulnerability plays a big role in my recovery today. To recover, I had to allow myself to become vulnerable. I had to throw away my armour and open myself up to new concepts. Vulnerability is not weakness. Vulnerability is courage, emotional risk, exposure, and uncertainty. It is the greatest measure of courage. Vulnerability is the birthplace of change. Without empathy, there can be no vulnerability, and without vulnerability, there can be no change.

It is my vision that eventually if there is to be any success in preventing addiction, we need to teach life skills to children at school. They need to be taught about toxic shame. They need to be taught about self-esteem and self-love. They really need personal development from a young age.

Similarly, when someone is arrested for drunk driving, in my opinion, it would be safer for all concerned if drunk drivers were automatically banned from driving once detected and required to attend a mandatory safety awreness course.. Drunk drivers need to be made aware of the dangers of driving while impaired, and in my experience that takes intensive training.

Chapter 9

A Message of Hope

For most of my drinking life, I could not accept I have the disease of alcoholism. I wanted to be normal and drink like most other men. I couldn't understand how a man could look at his watch, leave half a drink after him and say, "I have to go home, the wife has the dinner ready." I could never understand how they could leave unfinished drinks on the bar and walk away. I looked upon them as being weak. I could never do that. I had to get it down my neck until it almost came out my ears no matter how drunk I was. I couldn't understand why I didn't have the willpower to leave it and go. Because of that, I almost always ended up blind drunk and in a blackout.

I understand today that I have a disease, and that I am allergic to a highly addictive chemical. When the normal drinker consumes alcohol, it is eliminated at the rate of one unit per hour. The body converts the alcohol into a substance called acetaldehyde, which is highly toxic. If it was to build up in a person, they would get violently ill and die. However, it is broken down into carbon dioxide and water, then eliminated through the kidneys and lungs. This is what happens to normal drinkers, but something additional happens to alcoholics. Some of the acetaldehyde is not eliminated and goes straight to the brain, where it ends up as a chemical called tetrahydroisoquinoline, or THIQ as it is more commonly known. When an addict takes heroin, some of it breaks down and turns into THIQ. This substance is only manufactured in the brain of the alcoholic and addict and not in the brain of the normal social drinker. This chemical is highly addictive, and once produced remains, in the brain for life. It's considered much more powerful than morphine. This explains the powerful craving that occurs in the alcoholic or addict.

The more THIQ builds up in our body, the more we need and crave it. That is how the disease progresses. This explains the lack of control, once the alcoholic takes a drink. THIQ never leaves the body. By arresting the disease, it can lay dormant. However, if I pick up alcohol again even twenty years from now, that THIQ would be reactivated and I'd lose all control once more. That is the nature of this disease. I am now convinced that if I pick up alcohol again, it will trigger off a craving so powerful in me that I will do anything to get more of it. There is no known cure for this, except total abstinence. With a spiritual programme for living, it can be arrested one day at a time. I never asked to be allergic to this THIQ. I was like that from the moment I picked up alcohol as a teenager.

The American Medical Association declared that alcoholism was an illness way back in 1956. According to research, there is also a genetic component to this disease. Some people are born with an innate predisposition to becoming addicts, which explains why some people in families become addicted and others don't. What came together for me was the toxic shame, the faulty gene, and having alcohol at a young age. These all created the perfect breeding ground for alcoholism.

A Message of Hope

It destroyed the best years of my life and the lives of others, especially Paul and my own family. Although I now know alcoholism is a disease, there's not a day goes by that I don't think of Paul and his death and the injuries to his brother Pat and Michael the driver. I wonder if Paul was alive, what would he be like, would he be married and have kids? What would he have done with his life? It is something I'll never forget even though I have forgiven myself and stopped beating myself up.

I have learned to live with the Memories one day at a time, by practising a spiritual programme. I have learned that I'm not a bad person and never was. I did not set out that day to hurt or kill anyone. All I intended to do was have a farewell drink with my friend Mary in the local bar. If I'd known I'd had a disease and that it was unsafe for me to pick up alcohol, things would have been so different. Sadly, I was completely ignorant to that fact. I am now aware of my disease and responsible.

The disease lies dormant within me because it can only be arrested one day at a time, providing I practise my spiritual programme. Each day brings different circumstances and challenges and involves accepting the disease and surrendering to that concept, trusting that there's something greater than Slick working in my life—a power greater—listening through silence, having a grateful attitude, working on being unselfish, making amends where I have done harm, and trying to live a spiritual life so that toxic shame does not seep into it again.

The journey of recovery is a lifetime adventure on a road of hills and valleys, surrounded by beauty. Wakening up and taking this journey one step at a time has been the trip of a lifetime, an adventure inwards. I have learned to pause here and there, smell the scent of the wildflowers and the whitethorn, listen to the sweet melody of the mountain stream and hear the blackbird in the hedgerows once more. I have come to know the real Sean, who trusted enough to come out of hiding. I have discovered mountains of love, compassion, and kindness along the road, and every day I'm awake is a revelation of all the blessings bestowed upon me.

The greatest solution I have been blessed with and for living a good sober life is finding a power greater than Slick, and developing a working faith in that power. It is the only antidote to fear and alcoholism is a disease of fear. The longer I live in sobriety the less I can describe what this power is but the more I come to rely upon it. Through prayer and meditation, I continue to nurture and strengthen my relationship with this power. Without faith in this power I could not stay sober and live in reality.

The only way I continue to make amends to Paul and everyone involved is, first to stay sober one day at a time, and second to have empathy for people who have been through similar situations to mine. If someone causes the death of someone else by drunk driving and they have the disease of alcoholism or addiction, I believe they are victims, too, and through self-searching and total abstinence from their drug of choice it is possible to recover from the guilt and shame and live a good useful life. Every time Paul enters my head, I believe it's a call on me to reach out and help someone who's suffering.

It is my vision that by being vulnerable and sharing what happened to me and how I have recovered it will give hope to others and inspire them to come out of hiding, reach out and ask for the help they need and deserve. It is my wish that they will come to have compassion for themselves and come to a place of self-love and forgiveness and start living life once more. It is my hope they will carry the message of recovery to others.

Finding the Help You Need

If this book speaks to you, if you're thinking, "Yes, this is my struggle and my journey, too," I would like to invite you into a community of people who understand what you're going through. We are a group of people who have been involved in fatal accidents, caused by an addiction. We know the voice of the monster within that sabotages you forgiving yourself and embracing recovery.

Join our group, Alcoholics and Addicts in Fatal Accidents, here:

www.seanlynott.com

I'll look forward to travelling alongside you on the road of recovery.

Sean Lynott